THE
ROAD
I'VE
TROD

VOLUME ONE

LEGACY OF CULTURE

INSIGHTS FROM PAST
BAHAMIAN GENERATIONS

THE ROAD I'VE TROD

VOLUME ONE

LEGACY OF CULTURE

INSIGHTS FROM PAST
BAHAMIAN GENERATIONS

MRS. TERRY ANN EVANS BAIN

UNIVERSAL BREAK PRESS

Paperback ISBN: 978-1-956711-70-7 Hardcover ISBN: 978-1-
956711-71-4

Dedication

This book is dedicated to the memory of my late husband, Pastor
Wilfred Bain, my greatest inspiration,
and to my three wonderful children,
Wilfred (Willie), Krystal, and Brittany,
my living guardian angels.

Mrs. Bain's Children & Husband
Brittany, Krysta, Wilfred Bain Sr.,
Wilfred Jr.

Pastor Wilfred Bain Sr.,

Contents

Foreword

There's something about the way life used to be that stays with you forever—the phrases, the sounds, the habits, and the quiet, steady rhythms of a simpler time. For those of us who grew up in the Bahamas, the old ways are more than just memories; they're a part of who we are. Whether it was the elders reminding us to "carry yuhself proper," the laughter of neighbors sharing a meal, or the unshakable sense of community, the lessons of that time shaped us in ways we're only beginning to realize.

In this book, Mrs. Terry Ann Evans Bain has done something extraordinary. She hasn't just written a book; she's preserved a way of life. Through words, phrases, and reflections, she takes us back to the days when life was lived with intention, when respect wasn't optional, and when every moment—no matter how small—carried meaning.

For me, this book feels especially personal. Long before I had the privilege of working with Mrs. Bain, I experienced the impact of her family firsthand through her son, Wilfred. At a time when we were little more than coworkers, I lost my grandmother—"Grammy" as we call her in the Bahamas—just before Christmas. In the middle of my grief, it was Wilfred, someone I barely knew, who sent me a heartfelt note of condolences. It was simple, but it was thoughtful. And I remember sitting there, touched beyond words, thinking: He was raised right.

As a mother of a young son at the time, I couldn't help but hope I was raising my own child to grow into that kind of person— someone who would naturally choose kindness, thoughtfulness, and compassion, because that's what had been poured into them. It's no coincidence that those same qualities, which I saw so clearly in Wilfred, are exactly what Mrs. Bain captures so beautifully in this book.

The phrases and traditions she shares will transport you. You'll hear your grandparents' voices reminding you of values you may have forgotten. You'll feel the weight of their sacrifices and the strength of their wisdom. And you'll be reminded that there was a time when life was slower but richer, harder but fuller—because what mattered most wasn't convenience or success, but family, faith, and community.

This book is more than a reflection of the past; it's a challenge for us in the present. Are we honoring what was passed down to us? Are we carrying the same values forward? Are we teaching the next generation what respect, faith, and "broughtupcy" really mean?

For you, the reader, this is more than nostalgia. It's a gift—a chance to reconnect with the roots that ground us and the legacy that calls us forward. Mrs. Bain has created a timeless treasure, one that will remind you of the beauty in the old ways and inspire you to carry them into the future.

I am deeply honored to write this foreword and to share this work with you. This is not just a book—it's a celebration of who we are and where we come from. And it's a call to ensure that the values, wisdom, and culture of past generations live on in us and in those who will come after us.

Preface

The idea for this book first took root in 1984 when there was a national challenge to write a song or poem for that year's independence celebrations. Having intended to take part in the competition, I wrote a song, but never submitted it.

At that point, I began to collect authentic Bahamian material, and, over time, I compiled a wealth of memories and experiences. After all these years, I have now decided to put it in print.

The accounts mentioned in this book are strictly from my personal journey growing up in the Bahamas. The material spans approximately from my young childhood years at the age of six (6) and up until my early adulthood years.

The spelling of the Bahamian expressions mentioned in this book are subjective – as they were commonly spoken, but not written. Some expressions will be mentioned a few times in the book as they may apply to many different contexts.

To start this journey, below is the song I wrote back in 1984. It's titled, "Hands Across The Bahamas:

HANDS ACROSS THE BAHAMAS

Bahamians, Bahamians everywhere, Let's join hands and show that we care, This fair land that God gave to us, We need to preserve and keep it thus.

CHORUS

Come let all join hand in hand, Across the Bahamas our own dear land, Rid it of the scourges, Pray that peace emerges, Ask God to bless as together we stand.

Corruption and drugs are the order of the day, Let's join hands and stop their prey, This fair land that God gave to us, Needs to be purified and kept righteous.

Low morals, no scruples and sin abounds, Various diseases are sending a loud sound, God help our land you gave to us, We need to preserve and keep it thus.

Bahamians Bahamians everywhere, The call goes out let's one goal share, This beautiful land God gave to us, Is ours to preserve and keep it thus.

FINAL CHORUS

So come let's all join hand in hand, From isle to isle of our dear land, Rid it of it's scurges, Pray that peace emerges, And God will bless us as together we stand.

Introduction

My Parents: The Road Makers

On 8 March 1958, my earthly road began with humble beginnings as I was born in a small wooden house in a yard called Brown's Yard on Fritz Lane.   I was the first of eight children born to the Late Walter and the Late Violet Evans.

This small three-room structure housed a family of five. Ten years later we, now a family of eight, moved to our permanent home in South Beach Estates. The family eventually grew to ten people.

Though my childhood years were not filled with a lot of money or things, those years were still very happy. My parents were both Christians. My father was an aircraft engineer and as this job took him off the island quite a bit, my mother by her own decision became a stay-at-home wife.

She did all she could to ensure that we were properly cared for, supervised and trained with good manners.

From very early in life, we were taught things like "Yes Ma'am", "Yes Sir", "Good Morning/Evening", "Pardon Me" and "Excuse Me" just to name a few. We were taught to "say grace", to be satisfied with a "belly full" and to be generally grateful for everything we had.

With the family having so many children, you were assured of a new church outfit only at Christmas; and maybe Easter, if you were lucky. My mother learned to sew, so all school uniforms were "mama cut, papa stitched".

My father would make us draw our feet on a piece of paper to know what size to purchase when he bought our shoes from "away" - and he'd always buy them slightly bigger to avoid them being outgrown quickly. He would also bring school supplies, cloth and white uniform blouses in bulk and in various sizes - these never went to waste.

We learned early how to plait our hair, wash and iron our clothes and shine our shoes. We all graduated from the public school system and some of us went to college.

Our parents were satisfied at the end of the day as all 8 of us had good "government jobs" - every parent's dream for their children at that time.

Both of my parents were musically inclined. My Father was a sought-after soloist and my Mother an accomplished guitar and piano player.

During our family devotions, we would sing happily the many hymns she taught us as she played on the piano. Because of their life and witness, they saw the 8 of us make professions of Faith, and today, we are still actively involved in our church.

They laid a solid foundation for us built on trust in God, love, respect, honesty, hard work and gratitude for all that God has Blessed us with.

Mr. & Mrs. Walter Evans
(Mrs. Terry Bain's Parents)

CHAPTER ONE

Row Day

G rowing up, Row Day was a source of comedy. Row day is essentially when people with a close association (neighbors, coworkers etc.) have a strong disagreement and will argue as a result of the disagreement.

Row day could happen, for example, when one neighbor's child is playing and damages another neighbor's property (breaks a window or destroys flowers); this may lead to an argument between the two neighbors.

When this day came around, you stood around to hear what you could hear and see what you could see. All of your business came into the open, your dirty laundry was aired before the whole neighborhood.

Another common example of 'row day' is when a family member passed away and their assets had to be shared out.

While death can be a time of intense grief and pain, many family members are also waiting to see what they will inherit from the deceased. And of course, there was always one person who tried to take everything by any means necessary (we called these people 'all for me, baby'). They might even end up in court.

The eventual fight that would happen was 'row day'.

WHEN A ROW DAY CAME, THIS WAS WHAT YOU WERE LIKELY TO HEAR:

Still tongue is wise tongue
You made my life a living hell
You confusion making

You acting hoggish
Youse muck things up
Youse a sellout

You think you biggerty eh?
You head over heels in trouble

Carry ya gritsy teeth
Youse lie like a riffer
You couldn't drag my ole shoe
She was as calm as a lamb
You done sell your soul to the devil
They blow the whistle on you
She's make things up as she go along
You trapsy
You too like show off
Her head hard as a rock
Where there's smoke
You musse smell yasef

You make my blood run hot

Youse a bald-faced liar
You look like come here let me fix ya
He nearly take my head off
I won't trust you as far as I can spit
When you say A, she say B and back with a pose
You is a cutthroat
Ya mouth sharp

You ga soon see
I ain't gat you to study
Ya mouth hard

We ga buck heads

Youse a johnny come lately
They set you right up
You ain't gat no more sense than a land curb
Ah suckie suckie now
They rat you out
You look so dingy and good fa nuttin
You ain gat no broughtupsy
You could kiss my hips and go to ba devil
Youse a yellow belly
Youse a two faced liar
I don't back down from no one
Youse tick me right off
Youse a bare faced liar

Youse do everything slapdash
You like to jump to conclusions

You ain worth squat diddly
She wild as a cat
You look like ya own grandma
You ain't got no gaul
You look like a hen hard up with eggs
I don't know what this carrying on all about
He tell me right off
Put that in your pipe and smoke it
He give me a belly full
I leave them to God

You take that

She said a mouthful
You so slippery they have to sleep with 1 eye open
You bet your bottom dollar
You so brazen
Take my oath to God in Heaven and cross my heart to die
You won't be so fool as to try dat

9

MRS TERRY ANN EVANS BAIN

Shut the hell up, you still pee
the bed
When he turn on you fa true
You look like you just crawled
from under a rock
I ain fa dat
She raising hell up in harlem
You too like follow fashion
She don't play
You too like tote news

Don't run me up on brakes
Youse a scaredy cat

Don't cause me lay down my 3
Godhead
Kick up a fuss
Youse up to no good
I don't mince my words

Run along with her will get you
right in trouble
Youse a black sambo
Youse curry favour
You can't please black people
Tingum in da bush ain't gat no
name
I don't trifle
Still waters run deep
Youse a chicken ga lickin

I don't skylack
You gat diarrhoea of the mouth
You worship the ground he
walk on
She miff with me
You run me ragged
She throw a hissy fit

I don't take lowness from
nobody
You give me the runaround
Don't let the devil fool ya
Get from here with ya starve
gut sef
You so whatless
You ga hang yoursef with ya
own rope

You too forward

Youse run ya mouth like water
Gone with ya mouth full of lies

You too familiar
I know y'all partners in crime
You don't let things go
She stoke him right up
I don't roll over and play dead
fa nobody
She give me a sieve to drink out
You going to hell if only for 1
day
You getting old and cold

She carry me hard
You chicken out
Don't let me tell you how ya
sins arise
Bitching and moaning bout
everything
She want to talk hard to me
Outa sight, outa mind
You just like a loose cannon
Youse cloak them in
wrongdoing
I ain gat you to study
You better ketch yasef
He could do no wrong in your
sight
You ain't ready chile
She raised the roof
You cross my spirit

You throwing jeers
You got a nerve
You'se run ya juicy mouth too
much
You showing your true colours

You ain worth ya name
Youse run right out
Youse lie like a cat

Me and you ain no company
Don't put your hands akimba
round me

Don't raise cane with me

I ain't on ya run
You musse smell ya top lip
You musse think I born as big
as I is
Hog know where to rub he skin

Ya ma
Youse a slick vick
You dumb as an ox
Youse a chi chi man
Don't get ya hopes up

You too like play uppity
You ain ugly, you smoogly
She'll dash your hopes
You gat mouthatosis

You ain all dat

Who you think you talking to
He chew me right out

You think you all dat and a bag
of chips
You ghetto bad
You ga bust hell wide open

You better watch yasef
You ghetto fabulous

You always twisting things up
You need to go clean up your
dutty house

She as rowdy as they come

You look all broke down
You better stop while you
ahead
You musse wake up on the floor
They ga kick you to the curb

How you get up in that
You ga be ya own downfall
What you take me for

You let the devil get loose in
here
You can count me out
Who the cap fits
You shifty bad

Tell the truth and shame the
devil
Youse a snake in da grass
You like to sly poke
Well muddoes
You sneaky bad
You can't get out of your own
way
Well mudda take sick
You sin making
Chile you ain no use to me
Don't let ya mouth get you into
something that ya behind can't
get you out off
Youse the ring leader in all this
mischief
Don't upset my liver
You want me turn up my
gowntail fa you eh
You picking sin

You like big up yasef
Ya plaits sticking up like
bookers
I ain ga let you bum rush me
I mussie look like the ting with
the 2 big ears
You stay there playing the fool
Sticks and stones may break my
bones but calling me names
won't hurt me
You below my dignity and
above my speechiality
Don't cause me sin my soul
Gone with your seedy head

You think you thunderable
He so mad if you cut him he
won't bleed
Youse a cry baby sour lime
You really got a gumption nah
Gussie mae, gussie mae

11

*You really don't know your
place
He ain crack his teeth*

*She storm outa here
I see you there kicking up this
big fuss
You ain lift a finger to help
Rest ya nerves*

*You out here carrying on like
someone do you something
Good riddance to bad rubbish*

*Take ya time here
Chile I did gee her a piece of
my mind
Youse a pissy jew*

*She's tick me right off
You so sometimish*

*You like to play cute, only
monkeys cute
I ga sic my dog at ya
Chile I ain ga purge
You so good fa nothing
I ga give you piece of my mind
She thinks she's the cat's
pajamas
She give me the cold shoulder*

*Why you picking with me
You grasping at straws*

*If you don't like it, lump it
Big hole in your shoes/ socks,
begging for bread*

Gone with ya peasy head

*Chile please don't make me
sneeze
I ain't born yesterday
You ga cause me blow a gasket*

*Youse yuck up my vexation
I musse look like a market
donkey
The devil ain want you*

*You could afford to get up in
arms over that
Youse piss me right off
I think you make a bargain
with the devil
Look like you wan get up on ya
hind legs
She give me the brush off
I don't like how she look at me
funny
She acting cool with me*

*We had a big blow-out
They really take my nerve
She chew my head off
She row my head right off
You lookin fa trouble*

*You was the one to throw the
1st blow
Youse a lost cause
You making a Harry - mess of
things
I ga beat you at ya own game
I had her early told*

WHAT THEY DID WHEN THEY WERE TIRED OF ONLY TALKING

There may come a point in the disagreement where people would be tired of talking and would want to escalate things a bit more. When this happened, the following list of actions is what was likely to occur:

Break off running
Cuss me out stink
Poke me
Threaten to pop your neck
Pault with rock
Call me anything but a child of God
Lick out tongue and do bear
Wail ya behind
Sucker punch, bitch blow
Suck teeth
Give a good cut hip
Haul tail
Chap him up
Pinky promise
Bush crack man gone

Run away with their tail between their legs
She try lay me right out

Gang up on them
I gat ya back
Throw up ya gown tail
Kick in the knees
Don't take the lass
Goosey

Wail ya tail
Kick below the belt
Jook him up
Look like dog lost his tail
Sic the dog at ya
Buss out laughing
I ain no deep freeze
Youse a cry baby sour lime
Don't try to goosey me with ya big mouth
All you is, is mouth

You better haul tail if you know what good for ya

WHEN ROW DAY FINISH AND FOLKS MADE UP

Of course, Row Day never lasted too long. When it was all said and done, people either made up or went their separate ways. When this happened, you'd hear people say things like:

They just like 2 peas in a pod
They'll have your head if you talk about them
You better hold your mouth
Fly can't get between them
You out the picture
They ga high hat ya
You become public enemy # 1
They ain't checking for you
Drag your name through the mud

Youse an outsider
You better stay out their business
Mind your own business
Look for new friends
Trust is out da window
They turn their back on ya
Stop speaking to you
Talk bad about you
Go around handling your name to people

When Two People Have an Argument,
Emotions Can Clash Like
Thunderstorms!

CHAPTER TWO

What You Looking At?

As young children, we were taught that it was impolite to stare at people, especially if they were older. But we still found ways to observe the people around us. And, if we were asked to describe anybody, we were not short on descriptive phases.

For instance, I grew up with a young man in my neighborhood who had very large eyes. They would get even bigger when he opened them; so much so that he looked like a frog. Because of this, we nicknamed him.... Froggy! Froggy is just one example. There were many others who we described or gave nicknames to based on physical attributes, be it their size, certain physical idiosyncrasies, and even complexion.

SKIN COLOUR

This is how we described people's skin complexion in those days:

Black sambo	*Could almost go for white*
Black as tar	*2 tone skin*
High brown	*Tar baby*
Brown baby	*Hard red*
Brown mulatto skin	*Bleach out face*
Light skinned	*Mango skin*
Conchy Joe	*Albino*
Dark chocolate	*Black as a collie pot*

BODY COMPOSITION

Many people were given nicknames based on their size or body composition. I remember in junior school, there was a young lady who still had her 'baby weight' and had very large legs that would seemingly squish together every time she walked.

Because of this, we gave her the name "Fat Thighs". In terms of general physical appearance and body structure, the phrases below were commonly used:

Fat as a seal
She ain ugly, she pretty ugly
Big as an elephant
Look like Pillsbury dough boy
Big like binah
All hice up
Fat and slobbery
Rough looking
Heavy set
Coca cola shape
Look like a beanpole
You could see tiredness dropping off her
Dressed to kill
Look like come here let me fix ya
Dingy clothes
Look all beat up
Look all whapped out
Look like death warm over
All rig up
Look like he gat the weight of the world on his shoulders
I never see her look like that before
He big as a house
Old foggy
Look like jungalick

She top heavy
Look like a hully gully
Just a shell
She ain refined
Strong build
He strutting his stuff
Puny runt
Short and stumpy
Walk like steppin Fletcher
Look like 1 o'clock
Tall as a lamp post
Lok like he ain get another minute to live
Walk hip shot
Look like mutton dressed like a lamb
He boney
Look like he at death's door
Look like buggerman
Look like a gussiemae
Shape like a chicken
She look tormented

Wearing short of patience dress/pants/shirt
All hang down
Fat as a pig
Body size - she big and buxon

HOW WE DESCRIBED THE FACE, HAIR, MOUTH, TEETH, NECK ETC

If you said someone had a 'panny cake face', you knew that they had a big round face with a flattened nose almost resembling a pancake.

Similarly, most of the descriptions below are self-explanatory. We described people as we saw them. Some popular or well-known phrases used to describe people's looks were:

Frill lip
Porgy eye
Panny cake face
Plug teeth
Bumica head
Seedy head
Dragon breath
Bubby lip
Cock eyed
Nappy head
Snotty nose
Red head gingerbread
Big pop eye
B B in their eyes
High cheek bone
Chicken legs
Hatchet head
Goggle eyes
Nigger hair
Long gaulin neck
Calm head
Buck teeth
Picky head
Bandy legs
Empty mouth
Thick lip
Long mouth
Mullet head
Hammer head
Tie tongue bad
He does stutter
He has a heavy tongue

For for nose
Full eyes
Bridle round the mouth
Bubby ear
Cross eyed
Duck mouth
Spitty mouth
Big commolley on the head
Forky teeth
Buggerman in their nose
Chinese eyes
Arms look like a leg of ham
Sausage lip
Snaggle puss
Drop lip
Corny toes
Flat nose
Has a government gate
She got a hog style
Bugs bunny teeth
Peasy head
Lip dragging on the ground
Juicy mouth
Butt forehead
Full lip
Bat ears
Rabbit ears
Nanny plaits
Dungrow
Talk with a lisp
She does stammer
Talk with a heavy brogue

GENERAL DESCRIPTIONS FOR THE REST OF THE BODY

As a young lady you never wanted anyone to describe your feet as crusty or ashy as it went against the girl code of beauty.

Therefore, as young women, we always ensured our feet were nice to look at by scrubbing them with a flint rock and 'lotioning' our feet (heels especially) with Vaseline or Moroline grease. Moroline grease was a grease similar to Vaseline.

Some of the descriptions below could not be helped, you were born with them. Do you remember any of these?

Pigeon toe	*Duck foot*
Big bubby	*Big backyard*
Crusty feet	*Broad back*
Jelly belly	*Big pornch*
Left footed	*K leg*
Big boneghy	*Plenty gun cassen*
Skin look like he got barnacles	*You look like dead man walking*
Big gut	*You all hitch up*
Raisin legs	*She has cankles*
Legs look like 2 tree stumps	*Look like tingumsirmarybob*
Flat foot	*Full breasts*
Broad feet	*Knobby knees*
Parrot toe	*Knock knee*
Bow legged	*She look all jam – up*

WHAT PEOPLE SMELL LIKE

There was an elderly gentleman in our area who we called Mr. B. One of his favorite activities was walking around from house to house to "hail you". While his clothes were never that dirty; he had a very strong body odor – very strong body odor! In fact, you would normally smell him before you saw him.

And when he came, he would come inside your home, sit and talk for what seemed like hours. When he left, you knew he was there because he always left his scent in the room, on the porch, or wherever he sat.

I remember everybody who knew him endured this for years until his daughter moved in. She must have had a talk with him because things changed, and we were eternally grateful to her for the welcomed improvement in his hygiene. She was definitely an unsung national hero!

Here are some of the phrases used to describe body odor:

A pissy Jew
Rancy butter
Mangy dog
Like one big toejam
Rank as a boar
A pole cat
Dey ain bathe for days
You smell him before you see him
Like dry conch
Dog do do
He's a stinky pooh

Frousey
From here to high heaven
Outside terlitt
Funky donkey
Like a dead rat
Footsatosis
Ain no soap in their house
Water never touch his skin since he born
Man- o war sailor
Like a cesspit
Like a bag of onions

People Watching

CHAPTER THREE

Ring Play

Game time was our favorite activity during recess (lunch time) at school and/or our free time at home.

These times unknowingly taught us many life lessons. We learned dancing, cooperation, teamwork, how to have fun, the joy of laughter, mutual respect and how to build good friendships.

Most of the time, we were left unsupervised by the adults, they allowed us to play and have fun.

Most of the toys were self-made using things found around the house, in the yard, or in the bush.

GAMES WE PLAYED

Here are some of the games we played. How many of these do you remember?

Hoola hoop (usually a rim from an old bicycle)
Scooter (made from wood and 2 small tricycle tires)
Play dashing (future sumo wrestlers)
Jack stones (played with 6 small rocks and a small ball)
Spin top (peggin)
Hopscotch (drawn on the ground using chalky rock)

Porking (played with 2 teams and a tennis ball)
Sling shot (made from the tubes of bicycle wheels)
Make cowbells (mashed soda can with small rocks in it)
Jump rope (any long rope we could find)
Sword fight
Fly kite (made with newspaper and flour glue)

MRS TERRY ANN EVANS BAIN

Make drums from old buckets
Chinese hopscotch
Fire in the hole
Catching bees, wasps,
butterflies (in old mayonaise
jars)
Play racing
Red light, green light
Rounders (played with 2 teams
similar to softball)
Play wrestling / boxing
Play church
Cards (knuckles, spades, 21)
Hide and seek
Turn over catguts or head
foamus (our form of
gymnastics)
Play horsey
Duck, duck, goose
Box cart (made from discarded
wood and small tricycle tires)

I spy
Ring play
Ole mama how ya feeling

Play doctor
Play cricket
Dolly house
Shoot marbles (ring, guts, tar,
sizey,compurley, sizey/guppy,
stealy) (i inquest, I gee)
Simon says
River bank
Cowboys and crooks

See London
Hang the man
Play school
Tag
Spin the bottle

Sack race
Make mud pies
Swinging (2 long ropes
attached to a limb of a tree
with a wooden seat)
Tire race
Hoop race
Blind man's bluff

PLAYING MARBLES TERMS

I inquest	*Tar*	*Sizey*
Guts	*RING*	*Kitty*
I gee	*Compurley*	*Lifting*
Call dibs	*Slip goes*	*No lifting*
Cat eye	*No slunking*	*Come down first*
Shake no sound		

RING PLAY

Ring play is exactly what it says. Everyone gathered around in a circle with one person in the middle and then the chant began.

When the chant stopped, that person in the middle would go to a person of their choosing and make a "moo" (a shaking dance move).

This would go on until the bell rang for us to return to class.

Here are some of the popular 'ring play' songs of our time.

RIPE TOMATO

Ripe tomato green peas, how ya gonna sell them, lick dom bam.

PATTY CAKE

Patty cake, patty cake bakers man, bake me a cake as fast as you can.

JOSEY LICK

Josey put he hand in his pocket Josey lick, and if I had a mind like Josey I would L-I-C-K, lick through the window stick, oh Josey lick.

GREEN APPLE TREE

Round the green apple tree theres a person for me, miss lily, miss lily, your true lover is here, and he wrote you a letter to turn round your back.

TINGUM

Tingum in the bush ain gat no name, tingum in the bush aint gat no name

THE FARMER IN THE DELL

The farmer in the dell, the farmer in the dell, why oh acheerio the farmer in the dell

The farmer takes a wife, the wife takes the child, the child takes the cat, the cat takes the rat, the rat takes the cheese

The farmer runs away, the wife runs away, the child runs away, the cat runs away, the rat runs away, and the cheese stays.

PEAS PORRIDGE HOT

Peas porridge hot, peas porridge cold, peas porridge in the pot in the pot for 9 days old.

Some like it hot, some like it cold, some like it in the pot for 9 days old.

MRS TERRY ANN EVANS BAIN

PENNY SAUSAGE

Penny sausage here and a loaf of bread right there, take that penny sausage and stick it right in here.

CHEE   CHEE   CHEE

(slide push clap,   slide push clap)

Chee chee chee, I am a pretty little touch girl as pretty as I can be be be, and all the boys around my house just singing a song to me me me,

I L-O-V-E   love you

I K-I-S-S kiss you

I W-A-N-T want you

So darling I love you so

Dum de de dum dum doo dooo

Sha lah lah lah lah lah lah

LOOKA   THAT   BIRD

(slide push clap, slide push clap)

Chee chee   chee looka that bird, mamas gonna buy me a mocking bird, if that mocking bird don't sing, mamas gonna buy me a diamond ring, if that diamond ring don't shine, mamas gonna buy me a glass of wine, if that glass of wine get broke, mamas gonna buy me a billy goat, if that billy goat get away, mamas gonna whip my booootay.

I   AM   ZACHERY

Zim zim zim   I am Zachery, who stole the cookie out the cookie jar

Number 1 stole the cookie out the cookie jar

(number 1 replies) Who me??

(Zachery says) yes you!!

(number 1 says) Couldn't be

(Zachery says) Then who??

24

(number 1 says as he points to a person) Number 2 stole the cookie out the cookie jar

RED ROVER

2 teams stand facing each other, each forms a fence so that the opposing team member can't break through.

Red rover, red rover let Mary come over.

1 and 20

1 and 20, 2 and 20, 3 and 4 and 5 and 6 and 20, 27, 28, 29, 30.

1 and 30, 2 and 30, 3 and 4 and 5 and 6 and 30, 37, 38, 39 40.

FIRE IN THE HOLE THE THUNDER ROLL

OLE MAMA

Ole mama, ole mama, how ya feeling (x3)

WENT UP ON THE HILL

Went up on the hill with the bucket on ma head, the road so rocky til my bucket fell down, rocka ma cherry 1--2, rocka ma cherry 3--4

LOOPY LOOP

Here we go loopy loop, here we go loopy lie, here we go loopy loop on the Saturday night.

ROUND AND ROUND THE GARDEN

Round and round the garden like a teddy bear, 1 step, 2 step, tickle under there.

RING AROUND THE ROSES

Ring around the roses a pocket full of posies, atisha, atisha, we all fall down'

SUZY IN THE BAND

Suzy in the band John Demeritte, prettiest girl I ever did see, oh band, band arms around me play like Suzy gonna marry me,   so step of girl don't you come near me all those sassy words you say, so band, band arms around me play like Suzy gonna marry me.

THIS IS THE WAY YOU BELLABY (STUDIO)

This the way you bellaby, bellaby, bellaby, this the way you bellaby all night long, so step back sassy just like a lassy, so step back sassy all night long. Stepping through the alley, alley, alley, stepping through the alley all night long. So here comes the other one just like the other one, here comes the other one all night long.

TO THE LEFT, TO THE RIGHT, STAND UP SIT DOWN THAT'S ALRIGHT.

MA CHIREN, MA CHIREN

Ma chiren, Ma chiren yes mam, you hear me calling? yes mam. Why you don't come? / I don't feel like coming . I ga send my dog at ya........I don't care. I ga send my cat at ya......I don't care (run after them)

SHAKE THE DILLY TREE DILLY DROP, WHEN THE DILLY DROP PICK IT UP

MAN TAKE ONE AND SATISFY, WOMAN TAKE TWO AND SHE MAKE A MOO.

MAMA MA BELLY

Mama ma belly ga hut ma, call for the doctor to cure ma, doctor gave me an injection, injection to fight the infection'

THIS OLD MAN

This old man, he played I, he played knick knack on my drum, with a knick knick paddy wack give a dog a bone, this ole man came rolling home.

This ole man he played 2--shoe, 3--knee, 4--door, 5--hive, 6--sticks, 7--heaven, 8--gate, 9--line, 10---pen.

BLUE BIRD

Blue bird blue bird through my window (3 times), oh Johnny I'm tired, just take a little tap right right onto my shoulder (3 times), oh Johnny I'm tired.

26

LONDON BRIDGE

London bridge is falling down, falling down, falling down. London bridge is falling down, my fair lady.

London bridge is half built up, half built up, half built up. London bridge is all built up

Catch the one that comes through last, my fair lady.

SHOO FLY

Shoo fly don't bother me, shoo fly don't bother me, shoo fly don't bother me, I belong to somebody. I feel, I feel, I feel like a morning star, I belong to somebody.

R=A=T=T=L=E   S=N=A=K=E

Stands for rattle snake.

CHITTY,   CHITTY,   BANG,   BANG

Chitty chitty bang bang sitting on the wall, trying to make a dollar out of fifty cents. She miss, she miss, she miss like this.

I LOVE COFFEE, I LOVE TEA, I LOVE THE PRETTY GIRL WHO LOVES ME.

GOT A LETTER

Got a letter from Miami on the way I dropped it, a little girl who picked it up and put it in her pocket. Drip, drop, drop it.

LETTER FROM MIAMI

Got a letter from Miami, in the letter was a dollar, took the dollar, buy some candy, took the candy to a lady. Keep on loving me never stop, when the dollar drop pick it up. (x2)

MY MOTHER

My mother died and buried, my father forsake me not, I had no one to love me so they throw me in the deep blue sea, alapalachickengalala, alapala pooh.

BLUE HILL WATER DRY

Blue hill water dry, I know when to wash my clothes, I remember one saturday night, fried fish and johnny cake, alapalchickencalala alapalpooh.

JOHN JOHN THE BARBER WENT TO SHAVE HIS FATHER, THE RAZOR SLIP AND CUT HIS NECK, JOHN JOHN THE BARBER.

FLIES IN THE BUTTERMILK 2 BY 2, 2X2, 2X2,, FLIES IN THE BUTTERMILK 2X2, SKIP TO MA LOU MY DARLING.

HORSEY IN THE CARRIAGE GIDDY GIDDY GUP, NANNY IN THE ROAD AND HE CAN'T PICK IT UP.

MAMA LITTLE BABY LIKE SHORTNING, SHORTNING, MAMA LITTLE BABY LIKE SHORTNING BREAD.

DOWN, DOWN, BABY

Down , down baby, down by the riverside, sweet sweet baby don't ever let me die,chimey, chimey baby, chimey, chimey cocoaplum, that's all over down by the riverside.

MY BOSOM FRIEND IS BACK AGAIN I HAVEN'T SEEN YOU FOR TWO LONG YEARS AND GOD KNOWS IT.

A HUNTING WE WILL GO, A HUNTING WE WILL GO, WE'LL CATCH A FOX AND PUT HIM IN A BOX AND NEVER LET HIM GO.

PUNCHINELLA

Oh what can you do punchinella forty fella, what can you do punchinella forty two.

Oh we can do it too punchinella forty fella, we can do it too punchinella forty two

Who do you choose punchinella forty fella, who do you choose punchinella forty two.

HOKEY POKEY

You put your right foot in you take your right foot out (X2), and you shake it all about, you do the hokey pokey and you turn yourself around, that's what it's all about

Left foot in

Right arm in

Left arm in

BROWN GIRL IN THE RING

There's a brown girl in the ring fa la la la la la (X3)

And she looks like a sugar in a plum, plum,, plum.

Go look for your lover fa la la la la la (X3)

Go show me ya motion fa la la la la la la (X3)

And she looks like a sugar in a plum, plum, plum.

CENTIPEDE KNOCK TO MA DOLLAR, JOHNNY TAKE IT BACK, JOHNNY SLAM BAM.

HEADS   AND   SHOULDER

Heads and shoulder, baby 1, 2,   3 (x2) Heads and shoulder, heads and shoulder,   baby 1, 2, 3

2) Knees and ankles

3) Rock the cradle

4) Kick the bucket

5) Round the world

BOBBY BINGO

There was a farmer had a dog, his name is Bobby Bingo

B--I--N--G--O (x3) his name is Bobby Bingo

WHAT ARE LITTLE GIRLS/BOYS MADE OF

What are little girls made of (x2)

Sugar and spice and everything nice

That's what little girls are made of.

What are little boys made of (x2)

Snips and snails and puppy dog tails

That's what little boys are made of.

THIS LITTLE PIGGY

This little piggy went to market, this little piggy stayed at home,

This little piggy had roast beef, this little piggy had none,

This little piggy cried wee, wee, wee I can't find my way home.

HEADS AND SHOULDERS

Heads and shoulders, knees and toes (x3)

Heads and shoulders knees and toes, eyes, ears, mouth, and nose.

Of all my mother's children, I love myself the best

And when I get my belly full, I don't care bout the rest.

Ring Play using hola   Spinning Tops
hoops & marbles

CHAPTER FOUR

Where You Just Coming From?

Young children (then and now) were often sent on errands and were expected to be back within a specified time. When being sent out, you would hear things like "make haste" and "watch where ya going" as you were leaving. If you took too long to return, you had better have a good excuse or else! (Please refer to Chapter 5 for what "or else" may entail).

Me and my siblings would often be sent to the shop, which would normally take five minutes.

If those errands took longer than that, we would definitely hear "Where you just coming from?" And you better believe an unsatisfactory answer would lead to an unpleasant result.

When asked "Where you just coming from?", you were likely to hear one or more of the phrases below:

The dump tin	*From out da pineyard*
From collecting top	*To the Fort Hill*
From street meeting	*To catch one number*
It's day clean	*I get lock up*
From the wash house	*On the bay*
Catching crabs	*To the old homestead*
To buy a dream book	*From stretching ma legs*
It's 4 day in the morning	*I had a operation*
Down by the coppit	*I been spillagating*
Catching gapsee	*I been on the crazy hill*
Been to clear ma head	*Down the tract road*
I been on the contract	*To run some errands*
From the milk stand	*From watching the parade*

To the clinic
To catch masef
I just come from the states
From the petty shop
To pay the light bill
From the show

Send me on a wild goose chase
From off the jitney
From the club
Down the base road
To the dressmaker
From out the field
From the dance
From the post
To the barber
From sqashing out some clothes
From catching soldier crab
From in town
To get my shots
Just knock off
Gone for plait
From the hospital
In the bush
From the setting up
From the mill
From the dock
From the packing house
From catching a lift
From the mailboat
For my pension
Round the corner
From the island
From over the bridge
From the bank
Drug store
From confessional
From the farmers market
From the ice house

I been fishing
Through the short cut
To the hairdresser
From government ground
From the pink porch
From catching bees / wasp / butterflies
Over the hill
To the doctor to sound me
From the mailboat
From helping my friend out
Down to the well
Shooting pigeons
Through the dirt road
From the straw market
From the pond
Gone to throw my asue hand

Gone for wood for the stove
From down Bay Street
From the pump
From getting my asue draw
From over the hill
I been to vote
Been for a check up
From the fish house
From Farm road
I been campaigning
To get my teeth pull
From the produce exchange
It's pitch dark
I been to the PLP/ FNM rally
I ain put my foot out da house
You buss right up
From the swimming hole
From the creek
From spear fishing
From round the chicken coop
From Aunt Lizzies porch
From the salt pond

Public Water Pump

CHAPTER FIVE

Spare The Rod

Discipline, respect and manners were high priorities for parents when raising their children. It was a disgrace for people to refer to your children as "rude" and "no-manners".

Early on in life as children, we knew and learned the expected code of behaviour otherwise, we'd have to suffer the consequences – and no one was excluded. If you violated this code, the rod of correction was applied to your seat of learning.

Discipline was twofold and included a) what your parents said to you (row and threats) and b) what your parents did (spanking, restrictions etc.).

Besides your parents, discipline might be given by the teacher, the next-door neighbour, any older person, the pastor and the usher in church – just to name a few. Automatic authority was given to Grandparents, uncles and aunts.

In those days, if one was to do something wrong, especially where others saw, the news would reach home before you. You'd then come home to a stern talking to and a warm belt or switch. It truly was a village raising children back then.

During our primary school years corporal punishment was the order of the day. If the teacher had to give you "licks" for something you did, one of your classmates would always tell a younger or older sibling.

They would always get home before you and inform your mother. This often resulted in a second round of "licks".

Our parents would often say that you should only be warned once by the teacher. A second warning was unacceptable.

To avoid this, you had to bribe your sibling with "hush" treats or money. Younger siblings would take the bounty and still rat you out later on or when convenient for them.

WHAT YOUR PARENTS SAID

If you found yourself suffering the consequences for violating the established code of behaviour, you would hear one or more of the phrases below:

Who learn you them manners

I'll KNOCK THE stuffing out of you
I'll knock you where the sun don't shine
You look like you want to taste the cat-o nine tails
Go get the switch (tamarind preferably)
You on the road to destruction
The devil is a liar
You headed down the wrong path
I ga tan your behind
I'll slap your face twist
Didn't I tell you look but don't touch
I ain cloaking you in wrongdoing
If you can't hear you ga feel
You too cheeky

You fit a good cut hip (hide, tail, behind, skin)
Who you backtalking to?

You better not raise your voice/hand to me
I ain bring you up like that

I have to bend this tree while it is young
One good slap
Your hands too fast
If you don't change, dog eat ya lunch
You too womanish
I ga tan your hide
Hard head nuts don't make good soup
God charge me if I let you get away with this
You too foppish
I opening up a can of whop a**

36

I ga beat ya skin off
I brought you in this world and
I sure could take you out
You does pay bills round here?
Your head hard
You barking up the wrong tree
You tink you is man eh?
I ain heffin you up in no wrong doing
He does act too mannish for his age
Lord, give me the faith of Job
I ga tear up your behind
Sense and manners take you through the world
You ga soon know why lobster tail red
Fix ya face
Youse get right out ya skin
You really let me down
Watch your mouth now
I'll knock the living daylights out ya
Only one man and one woman in this house
I cry shame on you
You wan eat teeth sandwich eh?
You need to change
Youse one big disgrace
I'll knock you into next year

Your pa ga roast your behind
LORD give me strength
I does go to the end of the earth for y'all chirren
You look like you hellbent on doin wrong
I ain putting my head on the chopping block fa no one

Don't make up your face at me
I trying to put you on the straight and narrow
You too brazen
You does show youself right off
Don't screw up your face at me
Your luck raw
You musse smell yasef

Children are to be seen and not heard
Don't gimme no lip
You ga bring trouble on yasef
You cause me hang my head down
You musse smell a cut behind coming
I'll beat the black off you
I'll strike you down
I wash my hands off you
You better watch yourself
You look like you wan tote cut hip
You look like you want a screamer
You too spoil
Get the licking stick

I gatte weed out the bad apples
Youse a big let down
What I tell you bout keeping bad company
Spare the rod, spoil the child
Youse show ya tail right off
I tryin my level best to bring y'all up right
You letting your friend lead you astray
Ain't I tell you stay from round dem people place

WHAT YOUR PARENTS DID

And trust me, the above list is not filled with just empty threats – If a parent said one of these phrases, action usually followed.

My Mother, for instance, would often say, "if you wan be Cain, I is able", or, "I am the mailman, I can deliver."

There were actual consequences, and those consequences you might suffer would be described in the phrases below:

Tote a good cut hip	*Tap him up*
Pinch your skin	*Spank them up*
Lick him side his head	*Get grounded*
Row you out every day	*Make ya shame in front of your friends*
Box him up	*Wail your tail*
Wring your ears	*Shank them (hit ankle with rock)*
Tamarind switch party	*Look at you straight, no blinking*
Talk ya business to everybody	*Give you "the look"*
Beat on knuckles (for stealing)	*Do extra chores*
Wash out mouth with soap and water (for cursing)	*Give you the silent treatment*

WEAPONS OF CHOICE

I think that every house had a special belt. In our house we called it 'John Henry (or 'J. H.' for short).' He was kept in the heater closet and no one touched him but my mother.

We often laughed that J. H. lasted until the eight of us had grown up.

He was a symbol of discipline and respect and my mother never hesitated in using J.H.

Other weapons of choice were:

Belt with buckle	*Fist*
Fingers (pinching)	*Silent treatment*
Tamarind switch (all time favorite)	*Broom or mop (whatever was handy)*
Mouth (repeated rowing or telling off)	*Shoes and slippers*
Hands	*Gink you with a shoulder*

PUNISHMENT YOU WERE LIKELY TO GET IN SCHOOL

Teachers in school did not abuse their authority in disciplining students. For the most part, teachers were our school mothers and we carried fondness of them until we graduated from high school.

Once, when I was the nurse in charge of the Female Medical ward at the Princess Margaret Hospital, my 6th grade teacher was a patient.

Once she remembered me, we exchanged some pleasant memories of William Gordon Primary School.

She eventually passed away and I was deeply saddened as she certainly made a positive impact on my life.

Here are some of the punishments carried out:

Write lines	*Stand in corner on one foot*
Keep you in lunch break	*Send to headmaster's office*
Caning in hands or legs	*Report you to your parents*
Keep in after school	*Lose your "prefect" status*

INFRACTIONS AND THEIR PENALTIES

Each infraction carried its own penalty - some harsher than others (see below). Every child knew what to expect if he/she stepped out of line.

Therefore, if one often misbehaved and had to be constantly reprimanded, this person would be described as a 'glutton for punishment'.

We might also say that 'their head just ain't screw on right'.

The table below shows some common infractions:

MINOR INFRACTIONS

Cut your eye	*Not doing your assigned chores*
Long off your mouth	*Smoking*
Calling a sibling stupid	*Drinking*
Shrugging your shoulders in a daddy-may-care way	*Spitting on someone*
Rolling your eyes up	*Being rude to an adult*
Get beating in school	*Answering "WHAT" when called by a parent*
Getting caught up in a falsehood	*Raise hands (even to block blows from parents)*

CURSING

Cursing was something that most adults did not tolerate from children; even though a lot of them used profanity quite loosely themselves.

I recall there was a lady who lived around the corner from us who had a lot of children. Her husband had died and she was left to raise those children on her own.

She never remarried but managed to raise all of her children well and, as time went on, they all became productive members of our community.

We often joked that her big mouth, 'switching' (beatings) and cursing kept those children in line.

And if you can believe it, not one of her children ever cursed!!

Here are some of the words that landed you in trouble - some curse words carried more penalties than others:

MINOR CURSE WORDS

Blasted	*Frowsy*
Flipping	*Jack A***
Friggin	*Ya lie*
Durgin	*Cotton picking*
S***	*C*** sucker*

MAJOR CURSE WORDS

Youse a h*	*F**k off*
F**k	*B**ch*
Mother f**k	

I GA TELL!

YA MAH

The Holy Bible - Our Life Guide

CHAPTER SIX

For My Pension

Old age pension was paid out once a month from different 'Pay Stations'. The retired and elderly persons would normally collect their pensions from stations near the area they lived. Pension collections were normally a social 'meet 'n greet' time for the elderly.

I myself was often tasked with taking my Grandmother for her pension. She was always excited and wanted to get there early on the first day (there were 2 days of paying out) because she would see almost everyone she knew on that day.

Most of the seniors were always dressed in their 'good going out clothes' so people didn't think they looked all 'broke down'. Whenever I dropped her to the pay station, she would always tell me to come back in 2 hours to give her time to catch up on the happenings and have a 'lil talk' with her friends.

If someone died since the last pension date, everyone had to reminisce about that person and find out how the funeral was. Understandably, death announcements always made them sad.

When I picked her up, she always had a million things to fill me in on. Those people at that time didn't develop

Dementia like they do today mainly because they practiced good memory skills and paid attention to every little detail.

After receiving her pension, my Grandmother always had the next 2 hours planned out for you. She always took out her tithes first, because you 'can't rob GOD'. Then, she had to go to Portion Control and Sawyers wholesale to get her candy, salty sausage, cups, sugar, kool-aid and chips that she sold to the neighbourhood children.

She kept strict account of her money to ensure she 'break even' after her purchases. Her special treat to herself was always a 5-piece Kentucky Fried Chicken special with extra fries.

While my Grandmother always went home happy, I always went home exhausted and slightly broke after hours of driving and adding a few dollars from my own pocket to help complete her many purchases. Now that she is gone I often laugh at those times and cherish those precious memories.

CHAPTER SEVEN

Work It Out

Whether you worked on a job site or in the house, everyone had to learn a trade or some skill that helped you earn an income.

Additionally, it was equally as important that you teach and pass that trade on to someone else. We were always taught that there was dignity in hard work and making an honest living.

Given the way things were back then financially, once you had a family, you had to have a "steady job".

For example, although my mother was a housewife, she was also a trained typist and dressmaker – both highly sought-after skills in those days.

My father bought her a typewriter and she would sit up until late typing resumes and job letters. The added income was a welcome addition to the family budget.

My grandmother, who was also a housewife, was an excellent baker. My father, although an aircraft engineer, was also an avid fisherman who could rely on that for extra income should he have had complications with his engineering career.

WHAT KIND OF WORK DO YOU DO?

Normally when people met each other for the first time, their respective occupations would be a point of inquiry.

When asked "What's your trade?", you were likely to receive one of the responses below as these were the common trades/jobs people held at that time:

Drive horse in the carriage	*Making patch quilts*
Tailor	*Washer woman*
Work at gas station	*Fixing the roads*
Work on the contract	*House maid*
Shooting pigeons and chimney birds	*Bottling peppers, sour and tomatoes*
Ironing	*Drive tractor*
Mechanic	*Drawing plans*
Work at the slaughter house	*Hacker*
Straw vendor	*Bartender*
Keep a petty shop	*Dish-washer*
Truck driver	*Ice man*
Taxicab driver	*Barber*
Tote water	*Singer*
Mind children	*Gate-keeper*
Packing boy	*Peanut boy*
Selling "30 days"	*Dressmaker*
Construction worker	*Musician*
Preacher	*Sponger*
Farmer	*Stevador*
Wood carver	*Hairdresser*
Lunch lady	*Dancer*
Cashier	*Linesman*
Knitting, crocheting, smocking	*Crabbing*
Numbers man	*Fireman*
Hotel worker	*Marriage Officer*
Mason	*Plumber*
Granny - midwife	*School monitor*
Banker	*Prison guard*
Jockey	*Local Constable*
Diving	*Make coal*
Run on the mailboat	*Truant officer*
Lawyer	*Immigration officer*
Member of Parliament	*Commissioner*
At the mill (grinding corn)	*Plait top*
Sailor	*Teacher*
Doctor	*Customs officer*
Senator	*Telephone operator*

Janitress/janitor
Meter reader
Fireman
Justice of the Peace
Keep asue
Policy collector (policy man)
Stewardess
Drive the dump truck
Bark cocoanut
Curing goatskin for drums
Security man
Knead bread
Lighthouse keeper
Raising animals and chickens
Set fish traps
Keep a stall
Fisherman
Busting my gut where I can
Killing myself working
Breaking a sweat all day on the job
Tile layer
I still scrounging around trying to find something to do
Plait hair (flat and guinea row)
Welder

Burn flax
Nurse
Pilot
Fruit vendor
Dumpman (Garbage Collector)
Weeding yards
Painter
Newspaper boy
Baby sitter
Storekeeper
Carpenter/Joiner
Boat builder
Cook/Waitress/Waiter
Bus Driver
Hustling all over the place
Shoe shine boy
Collect scrap metal
Make crab baskets
Cabinet maker
I work the ghost/graveyard shift
Cure conch/fish
Work at the laundry

Build thatch palm roof
Work at the wash house

WHEN OUT OF A JOB YOU WOULD HEAR

Of course, it was not unusual for people to find themselves without a job from time to time.

Hotel and construction workers were often laid off when things were "slow".

When a person was unemployed, you'd likely hear them say one or more of the phrases below:

Tings ain tings
The Lord will make a way somehow
God help those who help themselves
Just waiting for my change to come
All buck up goes

Tings look like they picking up
Chile they lend me a lil hand

He suppose to be the boss but she run things round here
Try see if you could help me outta scrape
I ain gat nuttin to fall back on

MRS TERRY ANN EVANS BAIN

We living on a wing and a
Prayer
Ya really can't depend on
nobody
I hope tings soon level out
Feeling like a born loser

My hands tied

Work hard and ain gat nuttin to
show for it
I ain gat one penny to rub
against the other
I dog tired and broke
Things is slim pickens round
here
I gat to skim back on
everything

Chopping Down Trees

Tub and Scrubbing board

CHAPTER EIGHT

You Ain Hear What I Say Eh?

W e Bahamians have our own unique way of communicating with phrases that only a true son of the soil can understand.

We have been taught, learned and spoke the "Queen's English", but let us not forget our language heritage. It is what distinguishes us and sets us apart from other cultures.

We should be proud and appreciative from whence we came.

Let us learn, explore and evolve, stay on the cutting edge; but also, we should embrace what has made us a great nation before GOD and the world.

I hope you hear what I say eh??

ALL THINGS BAHAMIAN

Y'all skylackin you know
She ga bust hell wide open
She ain playing with a full deck
She believe she's the big bad wolf
Once in a blue moon
She living high of the horse
Having baby, 1 foot in the grave and 1 foot out
He's a gentle giant
I ain no fly by night
The devil let loose in here
I ain ga purge

Stop making sport
She sweet mouth
She high minded
She so wicked the grave will spit her up
You musse crazy
Haste makes waste
Let's get this over and done with
If you move you lose
She don't carefy
She so whatless
She vex as six

They bout the place handling my name

All she doing is knocking bout the place

What sweet ya tongue will bitter ya tail

She mad as blood

He just like a loose cannon

He's a scalawag

Look like mutton dress up like lamb

So slapdash

He so full of hesef

Yinna come here

Like play cute

He ain gat no heart

She was tickled pink

Gimme my tings

She got the whole kit and caboodle

The devil don't want him

Like talk old story

Youse a hot mess

Your navel string musse buried there

Kill 2 birds with 1 stone

Ain no use worrying your head over these lil things

I see said the blind man

He ain worth his name

He gone off the deep end

Hog know where to rub he skin

All shut eye ain sleep

He ain worth 5 cents

I don't trust her as far as I can spit

Chile I ain't ga take the lass

He wearing some big ole colonkey shoes

Talk is cheap, money buy land

He ain no true member

Chile don't hold your breath on that

She look all run down

Raise a holy kerniption

She making up for lost time

Chile she had one piece of carrying on there

The chip don't fall far from the block

I manage to scrap up something

Ain know their head from their foot

I don't play

He born way ahead of his time

Makecase

He so mad if you cut him he won't bleed

I don't trifle

He so happy go lucky

Tereckley

Shut mouth, no catch fly

You better get crackeralacking

She don't let nothing bother her

He spancil her down

Catching hell and calling it good times

All buck up goes

She takes life as it comes

All fun done

What's done in the dark will come to light

He meet he match

From hatchet was a hammer and chisel was a nail

You better ketch yasef here

6 and 1 half dozen of the other

I wish I was a fly on the wall

My spirit don't agree with him

You can't do wrong and get by

Like play uppity

He gat that monkey on his back he can't get rid of

Something drop in my spirit

They doing some monkey business

Like rig up stories

Family can't hide

Ya deeds does ketch up with you in life

Well mudda sick

This over and done with

She like to play hard to get

You could run but you can't hide

MRS TERRY ANN EVANS BAIN

Well mudda take sick
She ketching feelings
He does wear his heart on his
sleeve
Don't try to duck out of things
You half steppin
She does walk on her mouth
You can't take it with you
Your word is your bond
Get ya head out da clouds
Always raining on somebody's
parade
Her mouth does run like water
Youse a johnny come lately
You mind ya no good par
Always catching gapsees
Can't beat it with a stick
They ga bury me for stinkness
or sweetness

He so cheap and like to skinge
on everything
Take for granted
Looking for what you didn't put
down
You can't be serious
You ga get ketch in your own
trap
He don't know A if it was as big
as his head
Straighten up and fly right
He ain hit a lick all day
Everything honky dory
I don't want no bad blood
between us
Don't be watching nothing
Hard work never kill nobody
It sprying
I don't want you puttin any bad
spokes in my wheel
I have a sinking feeling bout
that
Don't be watching tings
You on ya own like Pat Boone
Chile y'all never see the light of
day with him
I keeping my mouth shut
He's a joneser

He real hoggish
I mussy look like a poppy show
Weghed in the balance and
found wanting
Me and you ain no company
She gat sticky fingers
Truth be told
I don't play with children
Her hands light
She's a seek out simon
Chile until you dead you ain't
pass nothing
Stay right there, you ga know
If you don't work ya ga eat dust
Like throw lowness
Once a man, twice a child
He gone fishening
If you don't work you will have
wind sandwich and water pie
for lunch
Blow ya nose where you catch
cold
He ain nothing to depend on
Dig one ditch, you better dig
two
You too high minded
He don't even know when
conch done
Don't have me spinning like a
top
Wearing rough dry clothes
What you take me for
Well I'll be a monkey's uncle
Poorness is no disgrace, just a
put back
Her dress bunch up
Busting my gut
You ga die bad
Where all dese people rack up
from?
Tingum in the bush ain gat no
name
Wild goose chase
Her head ain screw on right
He nearly scare the Bajesus out
of me
So far, so good
All up in arms

52

INSIGHTS FROM PAST BAHAMIAN GENERATIONS

*Make sure carry ya ferl in
ya bag*
*She back - back her car in
the wall*
Only God one knows
His mind get away from him
Put your John Henry here
Weather looks iffy
You ga bend or break
She all capunkled up
*Be careful what you let come
out ya mouth*
Bet ya bottom dollar
Cloak them in wrongdoing
Well blow me down
*You'll soon know why lobster
tail red*
*Once ya say something ya can't
take it back*
Blood thicker than water
Well mudda blues
Let sleeping dogs lie
*He ga throw cold water on
your idea*
*If you want to know me, come
live with me*
*You scratch my back and I
scratch yours*
You better look before you leap
If you live long enough
Too like slackness
Let the cat out da bag
She cross as a wasp
*Chile you cant drag his old
shoes*
Chile she acting up
Run me ragged
*Everywhere she go she always
causing a big combruction*
*Chile there's more than one
way to skin a cat*
She ain on ya run
*I right here between "Oh Lord"
and "Thank God"*
*She does watch people like a
hawk*
Stop corking up round here
Let well enough alone

*The minute he clap eyes on her,
he liked her*
*Boy if I didn't see it for
masef*
Bush crack, man gone
Nose outta joint
I don't like no mixing up
Can't stop ya ears from hearing
She in cahoots with them
My mind run across you
*He only get by on the skin of he
teeth*
I ga try ma hand
Boy, she don't let up
Play with fire you get burned
*You come too late you broke
the plate*
*He musse teef the church
money*
Live and let live
Long time, no see
Y'all joking
*Never see so in all my born
days*
*Tongue and teeth don't always
agree*
*Play with puppy they lick ya
mouth*
She does get besides herself
He cross as a bear
She like tote news
I ain't feeling to up to the mark
He like show off
*He'll teef lightning , and, catch
at thunder*
He'll dash ya hopes
Tired as a dog
*He don't know where to put his
self*
*She always letting her rice
singe*
Don't get ya hopes up on him
*I right here between Toby and
the dog*
*She get more out of life than
she expect*
Once bitten, twice shy
He was trying to out the fire

53

MRS TERRY ANN EVANS BAIN

This go round
He come down on me like a ton
of bricks

She bend over backwards for
them
Jump from the frying pan into
the fire
He like play big shot

Don't let nobody bum rush you
Stop flamming
You beat me to the deal
As luck would have it
He gone the whole 9 yards for
nuttin
He get swing
I at the end of my rope
Back on the side
The devil is a liar from the pits
of hell
She like crease up in ya house
He ga whip you into shape
He was gone in a heartbeat
I'd rather clothe you than feed
you
...catch me off guard
Pot calling the kettle black
She catch him on the fly
All you gat is ya name
For the life of me

1st rat in the hole tail covered
He ain polite, he perlitt

Life is hit or miss
oh really now
She miff with me
She gat more problems than
you can shake a stick at
You and me ain no company
Devil may care
She too like look down on
people
Ill be a monkey foot
Ignorance is bliss
He could run circles round you
You can't drag her old shoes

Y'all is jokers
She always putting her mouth
up in things that don't concern
her
He thinks he's the cat's
pajamas
He beat him to the punch

What you don't know won't hurt
you
Some people ain gat no grade
Ain't the sickest go the quickest
I need to clear the air
She ain no spring chicken
You ga wait til the cows
come home
Back over
Death is no respect of persons
He always calm as a lamb
She'll eat you out of house and
home
Chile dats an open secret
Chile you owe it to yourself
They gone right down
See like you don't see and hear
like you don't hear
She's miss know it all
I see said the blind man
It's as clear as mud
You have to wear people loose
She bite off more than she
could chew
He right in cahoots with them
His luck so raw, he musse teef
the church money
He fall down head foamus
He spin over catgut
Try not to dill dally around
What you expect, they ain know
no better
She's a ninny-com-poop
She off the hizzy-fa-shizzy
What sweet ya tongue, will
bitter ya tail
You think I was born yesterday
Take it from an old fool
She gone spill the beans
Been there, done that

54

She on her own run
He stubborn as a mule
She bossy
He real biggerty
Pack ya Georgie bundle and go bout ya business
She does go to sleep with the chickens
She cause it on hersef
She really rake him over the coals boy
That's why trouble can't stay from round her doorstep
A belly full, is a belly full
Dog eat ya lunch
Every man for himself and GOD for us all
She buss out laughing
You'll laugh til you cry
When ya hand in da lion's mouth ya gatte ease it out
Tingum in the bush ain gat no name
I ain ga purge
In the nick of time
He don't miss a beat

Action speaks louder than words
You favour ya pah, nah

She so big she can't get out her own way
Chile all I can say ya better watch ya back with him
Loose goat don't know how tie goat feels
They need lil sumtin to tide dem over
Ya look like buggerman

All shut eye ain sleep
Can't see the city for smoke
Dis musse spring tide
All livelong day
Sit small and wait til ya name call
You gatta fetch the best way you can
He really does do for more
He gat Niggeritis

Chile dis just a drop in da bucket
Give me a break
You don't eat where you pooh
Where you get your edumacation from
He so hully-gully
He really take it to heart
You could have knock me over with a feather
She always gat something up her sleeve
Still waters run deep
I soon reach
WHO make you judge and jury over me?
She send me to Timbucktoo and back
Chile she too highfullootin fa me
Let's get down to the nitty-gritty
She turn dem chairs cattycorner
School is kept and scholars attend
Man you gatte let us in on the grits
I ain see hide nor hair of him

CHAPTER NINE

What Ails You?

Whenever you met someone who knew you were sick, particularly if they were a bit older, the first question they would ask is 'what ails you?' or 'what you plague with?'.

Only authentic Bahamians understand these symptoms and you could be sure that they always had a cure.

Older people were very good at diagnosing your ailments, they would say that you just have "that look".

In my experience as a nurse, I can attest that they were right more than 95% of the time and usually hit the nail right on the head with their diagnosis. You only went to the doctor for a second opinion.

WHAT AILS YOU?

When someone asked 'What ails you?', you'd likely get one of the responses below:

My mouth keep springing water	*Teeth on edge*
I sick as a dog	*Blood poison*
I having weak spells	*Feel like I ga pass out*
Sores draining pus (fester)	*Crack my teeth*
Ringing in my ear	*Foot swellin up*
Heart trouble	*Belly bubbling*
I does have the weakness	*Her water broke*
Bumba flies around sores	*Burning when I pee*
Ketch a check	*My nerves bad*
She mix up like conch salad	*Body full of gas*

Feel like my stomach ga drop out
Getting up in age
Got the shakes
I get jook with nail
Screwing pain in my stomach
Got the colic
Hang toe nail
My nose stuffy
Get a rush of heat come over me
Heart beating right out my body
Night fever
I just had my teeth pull
Feeling nervousy
Have this heavy cold on my chest
Buck my toe
Eyes running water
Break out in a death sweat
I throw my back out
Have a bilgy stomach
Have tonsil trouble
Feeling like death warm over
Legs does all cramp up
Need a good clean out
Head swinging
Have this hacking cough
Got the runs
Weak back
Keep taking in short
I feel like a dog
Ketch a draft
She cascating all over the place (vomiting)
I ain sleeping a wink when night comes
My legs does give way from under me
Not feeling up to the mark
Cramp up
My wrist does swell and hurt when I eat ham
I does feel weak in the knees
Feeling under the weather
Lost his marbles
My head pounding

Puking - ain keeping nothing down
Bringing up plenty cold(mucus)
I believe somebody fix me
Stomach griping
Eye seeing double
Feel like I wan puke
Somebody hurted her
She talking out her head
I eat something that didn't agree with me
Them ropy veins on ma leg hurting
Seeing ma health too much
Her head bad
My teeth shocking
Dry cough and ain bringing up nothing
Going through the changes
She ain playing with a full deck
I have low blood
Choking cough
He little off
He's suck finger
Nose all block up
Somebody put mouth on you
Head ain screw on right
He's suck his tongue
I throw my guts up
Feeling giddy
Feeling out of sorts
I falling all away
Had to take life water / drip
Belly running
Every time I move I feel my bones crack
I gat a fish bone stuck in my throat
Feeling between "oh Lord and Thank God"
I pouring like a tap
I have a stiff neck
Right here between Toby and the dog
Spicy foods don't agree with me
I feel like I have the tissick
Runny nose
Someone work obeah on her

MRS TERRY ANN EVANS BAIN

I ain gat no mind to eat and I
falling all away
Feeling so so
Eye jumping
My eyes seeing lil flies
I can't stop hawking and
spitting all over the place
He doting
He gat the thing
Heaviness in my legs
Shooting pains all through my
body

Gat a sick stomach
Gone balistic
My nose all clog up
I can't see good when night
comes
Ma belly loose
She has fireballs (fibroids)
My teeth shakey
Ma toes and fingers feeling
numb
My throat feel like it closing up
on me
High blood
Need someone to tend to her

I so painful I don't know where
to put myself
I fall over the banister railing
Got sugar
Not feeling too spooty
I all bound up
I get scald with hot water
Got consumption
I so painful even my hair
hurting
He gat a roasting fever
I get plopped with chicken fat
He gat lock jaw
I feeling my age
The fever so hot you could fry
an egg on her
I does have the fits

I can't eat too late, the food
does stay in my chest
I keep having the dropsey
Got the agger
Breaking wind fast
I have gas in the front and back
passage
I have a hang nail
Got the flux
She over the hill
When my bowels too tight they
does drop out when I have a
pass
Stoppage in the pee
Hard of hearing
Toe jam
I itching all over til I scratch
myself in holes
I got a pain round my nabel
Blind as a bat
Bad corn on her toes
I get a deodorant lump under
my arms
I know when it's going to rain
cuz my joints hurt
Got a rash all over
My ears them get burn from the
straightening comb
My feet does swell up like 2
loaves of bread
My bowels tight
Her cut turn out
The perm burn up all my scalp
Got the belly
I can't get a pass
Something eating up her blood
I hurting all over like the
dickins
Ear rake (ear ache)
My breath cutting
Sticking pain in my side
I get poke in my eye
Some lye miss and get on my
hand
My bowels loose

TALKING ABOUT DEATH

Sadly, sometimes the symptoms would prove to be fatal and a loved one would pass away. Back then, we had many different phrases for when this happened.

Death would especially be a shock when you saw the person not too long before they passed.

When this happened, people would say "So 'n So died last night, and I just saw him on the weekend. Man, here to today, gone tomorrow"

Here are some ways we used to talk about death:

Throw crop, dead as a doornail	*Kick the bucket*
Food for the worms	*Playing with the angels*
Date with St. Peter	*Gone to meet his maker*
Here today, gone tomorrow	*Give up the ghost*
6 Feet under	*Bite the dust*
Singing with the angels	*Glorified dust*
Gone to the pearly gates	*Bust hell wide open*
Here today, gone today	*He cross over to the other side*
He's graveyard dirt	*He down to deaths door*
He cross the river	*He cross over Jordon*
He gone sudden, ain give no warning	*He was living on borrowed time*
She gone just like that	*Death is no respect of persons*

CHAPTER TEN

What You Could Use That For?

Following from the last chapter, when Bahamians asked, 'What ail you?', you could always be certain that they had a cure on hand.

One of these cures that older Bahamians were always quick to recommend was Bush Medicine.

Often, you'd hear the older people say, "The healing is in the leaves" - they weren't wrong. In The Bahamas, bush medicine has been used quite effectively for centuries.

Recently we have been seeing many commercials and podcasts by "Health Experts" promoting the use of natural plants and trees found in our yards to promote good health, this of course should be in consultation with your physician. Our older generation who swore by these remedies and took them all their lives are not surprised. They attest that these remedies have certainly been a contributing factor to their longevity and robust health.

Bush medicine was all they knew, and it has seemingly worked. They relied on this as medical help was not easily accessible especially on the family islands.

As a young girl about 11 years of age, I vividly remember a cousin going on a trip to Canada during the winter season and coming back with a "heavy chest cold".

She lost a lot of weight; her appetite was gone. She also had coughing spells which ended with her vomiting up a lot of "cold" (mucus) and sometimes blood. Everyone was saying she was 'consumpted' (contracted tuberculosis) and needed to go on the "pink porch" or chest wing of the hospital.

My grandmother and grandaunt weren't hearing that. They set out on a search in the bushes and returned with castor oil leaves, ceressee, bajerine, rooster comb, catnip, pondbush and galawind.

These plants were beaten and boiled in a big iron pot outside on a fire hearth, steeped for 3 days then poured in bottles after the mixture was strained. My cousin had to drink this poultice three times a day without fail for about two weeks.

After bringing up what seemed like buckets of cold (mucus), the cough gradually subsided and she regained her colour, appetite and strength.

My cousin, who we thought was a "goner", is still alive today and credits her robust health to that encounter with the poultice made of the healing leaves and plenty of prayers.

DIFFERENT REMEDIES:

Below are some of the remedies persons would give or recommend: -

Rub with lard to sweat out fever
Ebb tide of the sea for arthritis
Galawind bush for heavy chest colds and fever

Pond bush, lime tea for bad periods
Castor oil leaf for abscesses
Burn dry cocoanuts to repel mosquitoes

*Mother rests completely for 9
days post delivery*
*Castor oil leaf in hat or
headcloth for headaches and
fever*
*Salt water rinse after teeth
extraction*
*Say Grace over food for good
digestion*
*Lydia Pinkham tablets for
menopause*
*Paypaya leaf, raw garlic for
hypertension*
Flour pap for diarrhoea
Prunes for constipation
Guinep juice for toothache
*Ceresee, bajerine and banana
skin for worms*
Coal ash to whiten teeth
Pearoot for food poisoning
*Smoke pipe relives toothache
and upset stomach*
Boil croton leaf for cough
*Carrying baby low tie up
stomach to reduce pressure*
*Straw period - 6 weeks post-
delivery, no strenuous or
sexual activity*
*Warm honey butter and lemon
mixture for sore throat*
Hiccups matchstick on mole
*Karo syrup in milk for
constipation in babies*
*Avocardo pear for high-blood
cholesterol*
Cinnamon for heartburn
*Salt pork and copper coin to
draw out poison in nail stick*
*Hiccups - brown paper on
forehead*
*Florida water for fainting
spells*
*Orange peel tea for upset
stomach*
Bleach for ringworm
*Nutmeg in jaw reduce effects of
stroke*

*Meranga seeds for general
good health*
*Dill seed tea for upset stomach
and gripe in babies*

*Purple leaf periwinkle tea for
diabetes*
*Green alcohol for mosquito
bites*
*Neem bush boiled good for
building your strength*
*Ceresee, aloe and castor oil for
a good clean out*
Hiccups – blow on mole
W D 40 oil for aching joints
Beets to build blood up
*Cocoanut water good for the
kidneys*
Gas - hot lime or dill seed tea
Avocardo pear for good passes
*Paint house screens with motor
oil to repel mosquitoes*
Banana for constipation
*Gas - sit over bucket of hot
water*
*Bathe with skurgger needle or
sage or rooster comb for
measles and chicken pox*
*Eat crust of bread for curley
hair*
V8 juice to build up blood
Gas – vigorous taps on back

*Jumbey bush rub on skin
relieve mosquito bites*
Hot lime tea for period cramps
*Love vine and 21 gun salute for
infertility and impotency*
Gas - drink gripe water

*Relaxation and sleep use lime,
pear or soursop leaf tea*
*Hot water bottle on stomach
for gas pains*
Gas drink gin in hot water
*Red underclothes wards off evil
spirits*

Breadfruit leaf for high blood pressure

Phensic tabs and coke for bad headaches

Dip foot in drunken man's urine to remove sea eggs or needles

Dip head in sea water for colds and flu

Thyme tea and castor oil to bring on labour pains

Feen-o-mint gum for constipation

Sage or roostercomb bath for chicken pox

Smoke navel of babies for gas

Jackmadar bush for heavy headcold

Milk of magnesia to settle stomach

Pull teeth by tying thread to doorknob

Blow in soda bottle for retained placenta

Boil uneven number of bushes for the cure

Spike young child to young growing tree for asthma

Stocking cap for dandruff and sailor cap

Gentian violet for sores

Tie black ribbon on wrist if baby born with caul on the face

Limacol on skin for mosquito bites

Steeped madeira bark tea for general good health

General press of new mother after 9 days to maintain good health

Chew gum on plane to keep your ears clear

Raw okra, steeped madeira bark for strength

Eat pigeon peas for plenty of breast milk

Broad cotton waistband for mother's for back and stomach

Eat ripe banana skin to get rid of worms

Fever grass, baking soda for acid stomach

Honey on gum for cutting teeth

Broad cotton for newborn baby to keep naval flat

Pulp of orange (good for constipation)

Ginger tea, nutmeg tea for upset stomach

Boil shepherd needle for skin rash

Boiled rooster comb bush for heavy chest colds

Yellow elder and lignum vitae for heavy cold in your body

Gripe water for baby with stomach aches

Carnepe juice for toothache

Smoke pipe over baby's navel for stomach ache

Pistol from conch for impotency

Paypaya(paw-paw) leaf for high blood pressure

Ceresee Medicinal Plant

CHAPTER ELEVEN

How Much Money You Have

L ending and borrowing money led to many broken relationships through the years. When somebody borrowed money and was slow to pay it back, they were referred to as a "bad pay".

Many persons were unfortunately saddled with this classification and this dishonest practice generated a high level of mistrust for such people. The smart, prudent persons just knew not to borrow or lend money as much as possible. As Shakespeare wrote in Hamlet, "Neither a borrower or lender be."

For example, I had a relative who was known for borrowing money from everybody, but never paying it back – he was what many would consider a 'bad pay'.

What was even more interesting, he always seemed to know when other people had money. Go figure!

If somebody bought a new car or a new suit, you could rest assured that he'd be to their door before long stating that "something came up" and that he "needed a couple of dollars" and a little extra if possible, to "tide him over".

Before long people stopped lending him money, telling him that they worked hard for their money and couldn't lend him on slack knowing that he would not likely pay them back.

No doubt he lost plenty friends because of his actions.

POPULAR EXCUSES AND COMMENTS

Here are few phrases one might hear when it came to borrowing and lending money:

I ain't gat a dime
Like cry poor mouth
Living high of the horse
I don't have one red copper
They have more money than you can shake a stick at
He never work a hard day in his life
Ain want for nothing
They gat money to burn
He well to do
Like mooch off people
Put ya money where your mouth is
He's throw his money around
I only got a couple of dollars
Throw my hands in
Give with both hands open
You can't get a dime outta him
I could hardly make it
I have to scrounge around
Start from scratch
She does go to sleep with dollar signs on her eyes
I broker than the 10 commandments
He's a small fry
Start with bank account of zero
He sitting comfortably
Poor as a church mouse
I ga try to turn ma hand over
No one ever give me a dime
I skinging to make ends meet
Start from ground up
I ga pay piece meal
I so broke I can't even pay attention
I ain know when last I see a good day

Chile I dirt poor
Scrapping rock bottom
He loaded
They live on easy street
I don't have one penny to rub against another
Broke right down to the bottom of the barrel
They well off
Tings tough
Cheapskate
Hit the ground running
I living from paycheck to paycheck
Some things dirt cheap
Money to burn
Talk is cheap. money buy land
I gat more bills than money
Things ain reasonable
He straight
Ain much in the kitty
I flat broke
I need to put some elastic on my money so it could stretch
She ain gat a thing to worry about
He set for life
Ain nuttin left in da basket
She gat money to burn
I just starting out
Money don't grow on trees
The kitty dry
He gat money like dirt
She too like use people
I does try to scrimp and save
I ain gat a red copper

I could barely scrape up something

These prices sky high

She watching things

I ain gat nuttin

In above your head
I right down to the wire

They counting my money
I can't see the city for smoke
He hang his basket higher than
he can reach
He strike gold
Her Pah left her fixed

Money ducking me
Like play bigshot
She big eye
She get everything when they
dead
Only God one knows how I ga
make it
Ain worth 5 cent
He filthy rich
She get good insurance money

We living on mercy street

Ain gat pot to p*ss in and
window to throw it out
He could make it

She get paid out good
Her hands heavy
Ain worth his name
She fix fa life
He left them plenty money
She up to her ears in bills

He robbing Peter to pay Paul

I musse have a dollar sign on
my forehead

Born with a silver spoon in
their mouth
He always trying to jew down
the price
Ain worth the paper it written
on
Things tough
She ain gat a chick nor child to
spend her money on
Slim pickens
Fat cat, lean cat
He won't give you a dime if it
was to save his life
They grabalicious bad
He alwys trying to rip someone
off
She sitting pretty
He freehanded
She'll sell ya out
She so mean she won't give you
time to die
Have it made in a shade

Hand go, hand come
They born rich
You can't beat his prices with a
stick
I need someone to grease my
palm
Squandered away every dime

Put ya money where ya mouth
is
He dirt poor
Money don't grow on trees
He like play big shot
He ain worth his name
He right down to the wire
They think I gat a money tree in
my yard
They need to slip lil sumtin in
my hand.
I busted and disgusted

A Wallet Full of Bahamian Money

CHAPTER TWELVE

Body Parts

Every family and household had their own names for body parts. Funny enough, most of us did not learn the proper names until we were well into high school, and even then we still used our familiar names.

For example, our family word for genitalia (male and female) was "dodo" and imagine our son's surprise when he found out the proper names for these body parts in preschool. He could not wait to come home tell us how the proper names of the private parts were the "peanuts" and the "jennifer". 30 years later we still call them the "peanuts and the jennifer." This was a source of much amusement for the younger members of the family.

REAL NAME v/s WHAT WE CALLED IT

Some names for body parts you might hear are:

Breasts / Bubby, Tits, Boobies
Legs / Logs, Tree Stumps
Stomach / Belly, Gurum, Gut, Ponch
Head / Noggin
Hips / Backyard, Butt, Rump, Behind, Boonghy, Backside
Back / Grissell
Penis / Doggy, Ding-a-ling, DoDo, Digalee, D*ck, C*ck, Hot Dog, Peepee

Testicles / Balls, Jewels, Moth

Clitoris / Man in the Boat
Teeth / Choppers
Shape / Coca Cola, Brickhouse, Gussie
Naval / Mimba, Nabel
Urinate/ Pee, Piss, Catch a Leak, jumbalie
Bowels / Interest
Vagina / Crack, Girl's Tings, Front, Cr*bby, C*nny, P*ssy, Hairy Bank, Cookie, Toonkie, Bread, Vajayjay
Toes / Pinkies

Feces / Stool, Caca, Nanny, Doody, Pooh, Stinky Sh*t, Catch a Dump, stoompah

Breastfeed / Nurse, Sucking Bubby

Menstruation / Period, Seeing Your Health, The Curse

Sex drive / In Heat, Hot Nature, Body Jumpin

Menopause / The Changes, Changing Life

Sex / Doing Freshness, Lil Piece, Grind, Screwing, Cooting, Getting Some, F*cking

Erection / Hard On, Stiffy, J*rk Off

Injection / Getting a Shot, Getting a Needle

Fibroids / Fireballs

Ejaculation / Cum, Sk**ch

Impotent / Can't Raise the Dead

Aging / Over the Hill

Pus / Fester

Vomit / Throw Up, Cascate, Puke

Diarrhoea / The Runs, Loose Belly, Take in Short

Abortion / Do Away With It, Lights Out, Sew Up in Crab Basket

Getting breast / Bumping, Cutting Breast

Lisp / Heavy Tongue

Ear infection / Ear rake

Teeth sensitivity / Teeth On Edge

Wide upper thighs / Gun Casin, Love Handles

Epilepsy – having the fits

Pubic hair growth / Manning, Growing Woman

D. T.'s (Delirium Tremens) / The Shakes, Seeing the Green Men

Heart failure / Heart Trouble

Renal failure / Kidney Trouble

H I V / The Ting, Buy the Package, The Wiruss

Alzheimers / Dotin, Second Childhood

Flatulence / Poomp, Fart, Break Wind, Passing Gas, Drop a Bomb

Gonnorhea / The claps

Constipation / Bound Up

Tetanus / Lockjaw

Prostate problem / Stoppage in the Water

Nausea / Sick Stomach

Tuberculosis / Consumption

Sperm / Sk**ch

Miscarriage / Lost the Baby

Infertility / Empty Sack, Barren

Nasal congestion / Stuff Right Up, Stuffy Nose

Tonsillitis / Sore Throat

Conjunctivitis / Pink Eye

Uterus / Womb, Baby, Sack

FART / He pomp, He taking a dump, He fartin, He break wind

Baby bottle – Bubbah

Narcolepsy – having the dropsy

Virginity – cherry, pig in da bag

CHAPTER THIRTEEN

What's In A Dream

To the older generation, all outstanding dreams had a significant meaning. Because many people always dreamed 'straight' (their dreams always came true), many happenings and occurrences were usually correctly foretold through these dreams.

Back then and more recently, many persons also purchased published books that discussed the meanings of dreams.

For example, a common meaning attached to dreams about fish was that somebody was pregnant. One incident where this dream came true was when my grandaunt had a dream one night about fish.

Sure enough, she came to later find out that her daughter was indeed pregnant. She also traced the date of conception to the same night she had 'that dream'.

Aside from dreams alerting persons to certain happenings, persons generally relied heavily on dreams to give them insights into the future.

As with everybody, one may wake up and not remember what they dreamed the night before. If you mentioned this to somebody, you would likely hear, "If you can't remember your dream, eat cheese as soon as you wake up."

Nobody paid attention to their dreams more than people who played numbers. These persons depended heavily upon their dreams as a way to amass their fortunes (or misfortunes).

Each one had one or more 'Dream Books' which were used to interpret what they dreamed about and give their dreams a corresponding number to play.

If you met one of these persons, they would say things like "if you only have one dream book, you ain't serious" (Many people may also remember this phrase from a Pat Rahming song).

Even up to today, dream books are still a very common and valuable possession to the number players.

DREAM INTERPRETATIONS

Here are some of the popular dream interpretations that were given:-

Fish / Pregnancy
Teeth / Death
Plenty food and people eating / Confusion
Fruits out of season / Sickness
Car / Death
Funeral / Wedding
Dead people / Good luck if you don't touch them in dream
Being held down in dream / Demonic Attack

Running / Impending Danger
Black crow / Death

Plenty flies / Death
Crying / Happiness
Sharks / Prosperity

Bread / Prosperity
Water / Holy Spirit
Snake / Enemy
If dead person is happy / They are in heaven
If dead person hag you / You are doing something displeasing to them
Lizard (any size) / Pregnancy
Floods of water / Prosperity

WATCH YOUR LUCK

People were (and still are) quite superstitious in The Bahamas. We had a way of assigning meaning to certain occurrences in our lives and grouping it as either good or bad luck.

One rainy day, my aunt was driving down Minnie Street when this big black cat sprung out of nowhere and ran across her car. She narrowly missed him.

Shortly thereafter, turning onto Wulff Road, she got into an accident and her car was extensively damaged.

To this day she says that the black cat running across her car like the way it did was a sign of bad luck.

Watch out for these signs and be careful: -

If you keep falling down / You gonna hear bad news

If cat run across you / Turn around and spit 7 times
Bad luck to break a mirror

Bad luck to walk under a ladder
Sweep your foot / Run away from home
Mangoes bear heavy / Watch for hurricane

Be rude or curse older people / Hand will stick up in your coffin
Be mean and take things back / Get a hogsty

Boy child looks like mother / Born for good luck

Girl child looks like father / Born for good luck
Birthmark / Mother pity or yearn for something
Born with gray hair / Good luck

Sit on the bed of new mother with menses on / Mother will be very painful, baby's naval will bleed

Sweep outside at night / Invite evil spirits
Bad luck to open umbrella in the house

Born with caul over face / Will see spirits
Wear clothes on the wrong side to ward of spirits
Eye jumping / Will see someone you have not seen in a long time

Hand itching / Getting some unexpected money

Sleep with Bible open / Good night's rest, ward off evil spirits

If you overreach in pregnancy / Cord will go around the baby's neck in the womb
People in families die in 3's

If you eat out of a pot you will never get married
If you imagine you see a rat / Sign of death

Have widows peak / Mate will die first

Hair stand on edge / Evil spirits near
Having plenty hiccoughs as child / Growing fast
Cut boys hair too early / They will take long to talk
Rain on funeral day / Washing footprints off the earth
Rain with the sun out / Devil and his wife fighting for potcake
2 people speak at the same time / Jinx

You will most likely die where your navel string is buried
Bad luck for someone to walk on your shadow
You will live long if you appear while your name is being called
If joints hurt / Rain is coming

If you think you see spirits shout / Ten, ten, the Bible ten
If pregnant woman stomach is round / She is having a girl
If a pregnant woman stomach is oval / She is having a boy
Burn the mattress if someone dies on it

Dress end turn up / You will be getting a new dress

If a dark mark suddenly appears on leg or thigh, it is a death mark
If a young child has asthma spike him to a growing tree

If you wet your dress in front while washing / You will marry a drunken man
If you go in the sea with menses on you will attract the sharks
If your teeth is shooting pain / Somebody is talking about you
Lizard jump on you / Pregnancy
If bird pooh on you / Bad luck

Bad luck to touch a dead person in a dream

Talk bad about or take anything of a dead person they will hag you
Spit on somebody's grave / They will hag you
If you born with open front teeth / You will lie or sing well
If you stammer / You will sing well
If child takes long to talk / Wipe their mouth with a dish cloth
If boy child has 3-month colic / He will be very smart
If 2nd toe is longer than 1st toe / You will outlive your mate
If you are born with 6 fingers or toes / You will be very smart
If you have plenty heartburn in pregnancy / Child will have a lot of hair
If a man eats dark soup from a woman, he will want to get married soon
If a mother dies in childbirth, tie a black string around the wrist of the newborn
Cover all mirrors with a sheet in a lightening storm to avoid getting striked

74

In Bahamian Superstition, Dreaming Of
Fish Means Someone Close To You Is
Pregnant!

CHAPTER FOURTEEN

About Sex, Love, Baby, Marriage

SHHHHHHHH!

As people grow from adolescence to adulthood, they would start to become attractive to the opposite sex. People would start to hang out and date and many who were friends as children, grew up to like each other romantically.

For example, in high school, if a boy liked a girl, or vice versa, they might write on piece of paper "Do you like me?"

Below this question on the paper, there would be two boxes; one labeled 'yes' and the other labeled 'no'.

In order to be discreet, the person would in some instances have a friend deliver it. The young man would be elated if the 'yes' box was ticked.

Then of course, if people knew that two people were 'sweet' or 'liken' each other, they would make a big deal about this. When this happened, you would surely hear the rhyme below:

Mary and Johnny in the tree,
K-I-S-S-I-N-G,
1st comes love,
Then comes marriage,
Then comes the baby in the carriage

LOVE TALKS AKA RAPPIN (SWEET WORDS)

Historically, men were the chasers and women were the ones being chased.

In an effort to endear themselves to the females, men would have lines they would use. This would be called 'rappin.'

Below are some of the lines females would hear: -

Pssst, psst (sound made between teeth)
Sexy mama
Hey darling
Hey honey bun

Hey baby
Hey brown skin gal
Hey darling heart
Hey sugar plum

Hey sweetness
Hey sweet thing in the can

Hey baby doll
What's up girl
Hey lovely
Heaven must be missing an angel cuz you here
Hey sweetie pie
What's happening
Hey beautiful
You must be tired cuz you been running through my mind all day
Hey sexy
Don't get wet in the rain cuz sugar does melt

SOME REJECTIONS TO ADVANCES

Of course, the guys were not always successful and would have to endure rejection from time to time.

It was a different era, but women still knew what they wanted and in many cases were not shy about their disinterest.

Many men walked away with broken hearts – the woman they wanted did not want them back.

When a lady rejected a guy, he would likely hear one of the phrases below: -

Chile please
Youse run right out

Who you talking to
I don't skylack

I ain on ya run
I look like I want man eh?
You better go sit down
I don't play dat
Boy scatter like batter
I don't know why you showing
me all your teeth for
Catch yasef

Slow ya roll here
I wouldn't waste my breath on
you
What you scratching in my
hands for?
Later for you Jack
Jump back jack

Boy drop dead
Ain nuttin happening ma bouy
I ain't your baby
I musse look hard up for man
What you take me for
What you squeezing my hand
for?
What part of no you don't
understand
She ain gee him the time of day
Cool out brother

Chile you better come stepping
right
HUH!!!!
Get to steppin my brother

SEX (BAHAMIAN TERMS)

Sex was and always will be a big part of any culture. Bahamian culture is no exception.

Bahamians talk about it quite frequently whether they are discussing their own intimate relations or they're gossiping about other people's frolics.

If you were caught you would never in this lifetime live that scandal down. As a young girl living on East Street an older girl from next door was found by an older lady with her boyfriend near a big fig tree stump on Wilson Tract (sparsely populated at that time).

That young lady is older now but still referred to as V** by the fig tree by people who still live in the area.

Bahamians have a way of talking about things that is uniquely Bahamian and our terminology is incomparable to any other culture.

If the topic of sex came up, you'd likely hear the following phrases and terms used:

They do the nasty
She gee him lil piece
*They get catch f***ing*
*He was s***ing on her*

He break her in
They had a booty call
*She give him a b**w job*
They in heat

They was doing freshness
*They get catch gr***ing*
*He was e**ing her*
They get ketch in their birthday suit
They was doing the dutty
He spoil her
They was spooning
Pop the cherry

YOUR REPUTATION

When it came to sex, reputations were spoiled easily based on what people perceived. It was particularly harsh where women were concerned.

Women were often referred to as 'bad' and the men lauded as 'lovers'.

Here are some phrases that were used to describe somebody's reputation based on their perceived sexual behaviour: -

He ain no good
She is as bad as they come
She's a car cuz everyone done ride her
*Stiff c*** ain gat no concience*

*She's a h***

Trust me he ain gettin nuttin
She say no with her head and yes with her toe
He had her frop right up in da open
She say she's a madonna

She loose like a goose

She run round so much she has a slack nature
Every man round here know what her 2 faces look like

She's a hot potato
She ain gat no virtue
She done been with every Tom, Dick and Harry
She may look easy, but she deep
He thinks she is a pig in the bag
She say she is a virgin
Down there is like okra soup

She slippery like okra soup

She done spread eagle for half these men bout here
She does drop her draws for anyone
She is the one who break down Jericho wall with her badness
If he know what good for hesef he wouldn't bother with her

He does run around like a fool	*I'd be scared to go with him cuz I might ketch something*
Chile she's a mattress cuz everybody dun lay on her *He done run round so much he done blow his fuse*	*She take the cake* *She as bad as I don't know what*

COURTING

When courting, the person you were "liking" was expected to meet your parents for scrutiny and to gain their approval. Their first question was usually, "who may you be" and secondly "who your people is". When asking about your family, they'd usually want you to go back about 3-4 generations to ensure that you were not related.

If you pass this test, you'd then have to state your intentions. When it came time for the engagement, it would be sealed with a ring and accompanied by a letter. This letter was kept by the parents; just in case the groom had second thoughts and tried to bail out. In this situation, the parents would threaten to take the young man to court and sue him for "Breach of Promise".

Grandmothers were also very discerning and had a sixth sense about matters of importance.

Often times, after looking a person's boyfriend/girlfriend over and asking a few pointed questions, the grandmother would remark that something about the young man or woman "trouble their spirit" and/or that "he/she isn't what they pretend to be", they could see right through them, if they didn't mean you any good.

They would then tell you that if you didn't heed their warning, you would live to regret it and would come to their grave to beg their pardon.

Let's also recognize that the Grandmothers were accurate and would be right about 95% of the time. They seemed to have a 6th sense about these things.

If all went well, and the person made it pass your parents and grandparents, the match was sealed, and your future husband or wife was called "your intended".

You were still expected to live morally while being engaged and not partake in premarital sex.

Living together before marriage or shacking up was heavily frowned upon - the older people called this "burning the matrimony".

If the couple were "smitten" with each other, you would hear phrases like this: -

They head over heels in love
She love him more than life itself
He frettin bout her and fall all away
She does act like he's her earthly god
He done lost all he senses
He could do no wrong in her sight
I believe she gee him some cuckoo soup
She worship even his shadow
She gat him wrapped around her little finger
She gat his heart in her hands
She gat him eating out her hand
She gat him in the palms of her hands
He'll sell his soul fa her

She cryin her eyes out over him
She love the dirt he walk on

He look like he's the real deal

She musse gee him nanny to eat
He cause her turn her back on her family
He can't keep from round her house
When he say 'jump', she say 'how high'
He can't ketch hesef
She in his blood

She so in love she in dog heaven
He lovestruck
I ain never seen such hot love in my life
He would kill fa her
He just like a dog in heat

He blow all his savings on her

She make him spend all his earnings
He didn't rest til he get her
When he round her he ain gat no sense
Her sun rise and set on him

He does look at her like she is gold
He give her a run for her money
He's her sun and moon
He ain take his eyes off her yet

They ain come off the love boat yet
You see one you see the other

Just like a lost puppy
He losing all kinda sleep over her

MARRIAGE

Most parents vowed that their daughters were decent and untouched. It was a tradition on most if not all family islands for the new couple to sleep on a white sheet for their wedding night.

The next day everyone was waiting to see if the soiled sheet was hanging on the line. If not, tongues were 'wagging' and heads were shaking.

The smart girls got married while they were menstruating. In some islands the groom was given a shotgun for him to shoot after the initial intercourse to confirm that his new wife was a virgin. People got up from '4 day in the morning' in anticipation of hearing the 'shot ring out in the land'.

You could imagine the "talks" if the gun did not go off.

It was not unusual for the wedding to be on a weekday, in fact it was almost the norm. Most ceremonies were held in the evening with a 'house reception' that followed.

The bride's family were responsible for securing the church, 'outfitting the bride' and fund the reception. The groom's main responsibility was the wedding ring, provide a car or carriage and find their new residence.

Moving in with parents was not looked upon as a wise decision. This is because most people felt a new couple would not have their space and privacy and everyone was going to be all up in their business and "put their mouth in it" and, take sides.

The older people would often tell the couple that you get married in ya "mind" first then ya "hind".

If a couple was fortunate enough to be given a house or 'piece of lot' to put them on their feet, it was a great start to their life together.

The couple was admonished to keep their plans between them and let the 'pillow talk' stay on the pillow and strictly between them two.

TALKING ABOUT MARRIAGE

When persons got married, here are the phrases that were used: -

Tie the knot
They jump ship
Had a secret to do
He get swing big time
Get hitched
I hear she ketch him in a serious lie
Put a noose around his neck
I hear he already gat sweet heart, quick as dat
They had a shotgun wedding

Chile ain nobody know when they do that

He get hesef a wife
He done gat sweetheart
He get hook in the bait
They barely making it
They jump the broom
They ain ga last as long as Patty last in the army
Gone to the J. P.
Their wedding was the talk of the town
They gone away and do that thing
They ain tell nobody nuttin

AFTER WEDDING TALKS

Just like now, people always had plenty to say after a wedding.

People would gossip about the people involved in the wedding and/or express opinions on things like the wedding itself, the bridal party's attire or anything else in between.

Some people just come to look to have something to talk about, and talk even after eating up all of your food and "toting" some home.

Most of the talks were to 'find fault' about the whole wedding from beginning to the end.

Here are some of the things that would be said during or after a wedding:

Her belly was really poking out that dress

Some people even ain get nothing to eat

I hear he like to fight

She robbin the cradle, he could be her son

He get a ready made family

Too much cartin was going on

Chile I hear she cuss his Mah out stink

She was so happy she was in dog heaven

I hear he was married before, no woman does leave good man

Her Mah ain put her foot to it

Them people was drinking and carrying on like yard dogs

I hear his people can't stand her

I hear she put everyone in their place

I hope he / she know what they getting into

That emcee was sure bursting their bubbles

Chile her people ain't particular bout him atall, atall

The bride mother didn't look fit

Her mother ain smile yet

Boy anybody could wear white these days

Chile he ain getting nothing

Them bridesmaids clothes was all hitch up

What a sad wedding

They say he is a whoremonger

I hear their family didn't agree for the wedding

All them chirren she gat and she wear white

They was whole 3 hours late, they think people gat time to waste

I hear they force he hand

Some of them family dress like they was going to the club

I hear she gat a child what he ain know bout

They running late and gat 100 people in the bridal party

He's a real man, he don't mess around

I wonder who cook that food

I hear they had a big breakdown at the reception

You could see the bridal party didn't practise together

If you wa know me, come live with me	*He don't take no foolishness*
The food run out quick	*He old enough to be her Pah*
When his ole galfriend show up all hell break loose	*Wait til the smoke clears to see how tings pan out for them*

PREGNANCY

Whether married or not, a pregnancy was and is always big news. If the wedding was a little "suspect", meaning you had to get married, the countdown began to see how many months it would be to the delivery of the baby.

If the baby came before 7-9 months after the wedding, the talk would be that she walked down the aisle "heavy right down".

Some mothers would try to defend their daughters and say that the baby was premature, not too convincing if the 'premmie' weighed 8 pounds, HUH?

The mother of the bride was her biggest defender.

Here is how a pregnancy would be announced: -

She spitting and throwing up all over the place	*She wish she could have a pigeon pair*
She heavy	*She knock up*
She big up	*She is big as a house*
Gern to New York soon	*She making page of her age*
She trap him	*She breeding bad*
She get ketch	*They making foot for socks*
She eating for 2	*About to go down*
She gat 1 foot in the grave and 1 foot out	*She gat all kinds of cravings, hope she don't mark that baby*
Hope she don't breed like a chicken	*Dat's the only way she could ketch him*
She decide to try her hand	*A little birdie told me*
Dat ketch her off guard	*She sure showing y'all a thing or two*

NEW BORN BABY LOOKS LIKE WHO?

A new baby always came with much excitement. Everybody wanted to visit the newborn to see what and who it looked like, especially if the father's identity was questionable.

Many years ago, a very near relative was having a child for a supposedly dark man who was 'well-to-do'. Lo and behold, at the birth this child came out 'very hard red' (lightskinned). My relative lost a big income as well as her reputation.

After people visited a newborn and its parents, one might here one of the phrases below: -

She ain lie on him	*She better go look for he pah*
He cut right off the man	*She blame it on the wrong one*
That child is a mini me	*Spitting image of the man*
Chile she do sum skullduggery	*He get swing big time*
The very man, the very man	*Chile please*
That baby couldn't look more like him than if he born it himself	*That child ain look like none of them*
She ain lie on him	*Dat child ain look nuttin like him*

AFTER THE BABY COMES

On all of the islands they is always a "Granny" or "Midwife" who "tends" to the mother after delivery to ensure that she returns to optimal health.

My grandmother, not formally trained as a nurse was a 'Granny'. She delivered most of the babies in the North Andros Area.

She boasted that she rarely encountered any problems, but, the women considered high risk were sent to Nassau for closer observation and care. These women were highly respected, wise and no nonsense.

The 6 weeks post-delivery was called "being in straw".

These women were strict and implemented a series of rules that were to be complied with – no questions asked.

A new mother would also have to face the music with a Granny or Midwife if they did not comply with their commands.

They would often say that your body is 'knitting back together' after delivery, and if you pick up something it will stay in your body and make you very sick as you grow older. Handle your 'one body' with care.

Below are some of the rules that would be implemented by the Granny or Midwife when tending to a mother who had just given birth:

YOU WERE NOT ALLOWED TO AND EXPECTED TO DO THE FOLLOWING: -

Do not come out of the house for 9 days
No cooking, cleaning, or washing clothes
No one sits on the bed
Keep your body well covered at all times (hot or cold weather)
Limit people handling baby, especially THEIR hands and mouth
Drink ceresee for 9 days to clean you out

Drink tea 3-4 times a day so as not to give the baby gas
Your body must be "pressed from head to toe" after 9 days to bring it back together
Can't wear high heels or tight-up and skimpy clothes

Never walk barefooted or bare headed
No excessive talking to give you gas
No bright lights
Mother and baby must wear broad cotton waist band
Mother Don't eat pepper or spicy food - it will gripe the baby
No visitors after 6pm, if after 5pm let the draaft fall of you before entering the room
Eat pigeon peas so that the milk could spring plenty
No sexual relations for 2-3 months

No drinking of alcohol while breastfeeding the baby

In Bahamian Tradition, Your Intended
Came With a Ring and a Letter to
Seal the Engagement.

CHAPTER FIFTEEN

What You Say Your Name is Again?

In retrospect, it was surprising (and a little funny) to realize that there were some individuals we knew all of our lives and yet never knew their real names because we only called them by their "nicknames".

It was not until a death or marriage occurred that we learned their real names. Adults were always addressed as Mister, Miss, or Misses, and were never called by their first names.

Likewise, the same was done for aunts, uncles, and other close adult relatives. 'Unc', 'Aunty' and 'Miss Veese' were all we knew!!!

For example, growing up, there was a boy we played with who we called "Day Day", a relative of one of our neighbours. We would see him constantly and this was the only name we ever called him.

It never occurred to any of us that we did not know his real name until he had a death in his family, and we tried to find his name in the news paper.

We looked and looked, but we were looking for "Day Day" which was not placed anywhere in the paper. We soon discovered, his actual name, was Hulen.

COMMON NAMES FOR CLOSE RELATIVES:

We had special names for our relatives based on their relation to us or their position in the family. My grandmother, for example, was referred to as 'Mama'. Below are some of the common names that were used for family members and close relatives: -

PERSON / WHAT WE CALLED THEM

Mother / Mom, Mommy, Mudda, Mammy, Mama, My Ole Lady

Father / Daddy, Fadda, Pops, Pappy, The Ole Man

Grandmother / Grammy, Gramm-mar, Grummy, Mama, Nana

Grandfather / Pappy, Grand-Daddy, Gramps, Papa

Oldest sister / Titta, Bis Sis, YaYa

Any Cousin / Cousin was always placed in front of a cousin's name ie. Cousin George

Oldest brother / Bulla

Anyone Named after Their Father / Junior

Any older cousin / Con

Youngest male and female child / Baby Boy/Baby Girl

Godmother / Goddy

No matter how old or young Aunts and Uncles were never called by their first name

ADULT GREETINGS

Children also had their own nicknames or pet names as well. Adults were generally kind to children and always referred to them with terms of endearment (buttering up) – especially if they needed you to do them a favour.

If they asked a chore of you they were very rarely refused after calling you "sweetie pie". Most of the time they put a little something in your hand to 'sweeten the pot'.

Below are just some of the names you might be referred to:

Hey baby
Buster
My beloved
Sweet girl
How you doing darling
Soldier
Baby doll
Empress
Stonka - lonkus
Bossman
Babykins
Honey child
Hey buddy

Hey sweetie pie
Honey
Homeboy
Prince / Princess
Stonka
Sugar
Toonka
Hey Bro / Sis
Bosslady
Sweet thing in the can
Darling heart
Chief
Honey Bun

POPULAR NICKNAMES ATTACHED TO NAMES

Often times, people's nicknames were a shortened version of their actual names. My brother Rae Anthony, for instance, is often referred to as 'Tony'.

Below are some of the common names people had and the shortened versions:

Rudolph / Ruddy
Sandra / Sandy
Bethsheba / Sheba / Beth
Octavious / Tavy
Pandora / Penny,Panny
Oswald / Ozzy
Georgina / Georgey
Dorothy / Dot

Richard / Ricky
Bernadettez / Bernie
Benson / Sonny

Patricia / Pat/Trish / Patsy
Elizabeth / Betty, Lizzie

Florence / Flo
Albertha/ Robertha / Bertha
Arlington / Allie
Malvina / Mally
Herbert / Herb
Majorie / Madge
Joshua / Josh
Thomas / Thomasina / Tom, Tommy
Deborah / Debbie
Lincoln / Links, Linky
Christine / Christopher / Chris, Chrissey, Teeny
Margaret / Meg, Muggie
Barbara / Barbie

MRS TERRY ANN EVANS BAIN

Cleophus/ Cleopatra / Cleo, Cleet
Leopold / Leo
Patrice / Tricey
Bertrum / Bert
Gertrude / Gertie / Trudy
Zachariah / Zack
Theresa / Tess / Terry
Michele / Shelly
Robert / Rob, Robby, Bob
Abigail / Abby
Timothy / Timmy
James / Jimmy
Benjamin / Benny
Samuel / Sam, Sammy
Jennifer / Jen, Jenny
Leonora / Nora
Jeremiah / Jerry, Miah
Geraldine / Gerry
Joseph / Josephine / Jojo, Joey, Joe, Josey
Tabitha / Tabby
Gabrielle / Gabby
Karen / Kay
Stephanie / Steph
Anastacia / Stacey
Prescola / Pressy
Magnola / Maggie
Carolyn, Caroline / Carry
Franklin / Frankie
Andrew / Andy,Dru
Alphonsa / Phonsa
Francina / Fran, Franny
Ismelda / Izzy
Katherine / Katie, Kitty
Lucinda, Lucille / Lucy
Ophelia / Offey
Patrina / Patrinella / Pet
Raymond / Ray, Mond
Kimberly / Kim, Kimmy
Phillippa / Philly
Victoria / Vicky
Maudice, Maudline / Maud, Maudie
Virginia / Virgy, Ginny
Roosevelt / Roosy
Maxine / Max, Maxie
Sharon / Shea

Wilfred / William / Willy, Bill, Billy
Anthony / Tony
Rosemary / Rosy
Melvern / Melannie / Mellie
Wellington / Welly
Jeffrey / Jeff
Eloise, Ellington / Ellie
Michael / Mikey,
Marilyn / Marry, Lynn
Bloneva / Blonney
Jaqueline / Jackie
Veronica / Ronnie
Matthew / Marty
Ezekiel / Zeke
Clement / Clem
Donald / Donny
Frederick / Fredrica / Freddie
Elaine / Leany
Valerie / Valderine / Val, Vally

Randolph / Randy
Walter, Walton / Wally
Nicholas / Nicky
Nicola / Nickey, Lorrie
Natasha / Tasha, Tash
Janet / Net, Nettie
Smith / Smitty
Jonathon / John, Johnny
Valencia / Val, Lencie
Howard / Howie
Bradley / Brad
Norman / Norm
Kirklyn / Kirk, Kirky
Spencer / Spence
Sherrilyn / Sherry,Lynn
Irene / Irry, Rainy
Agnes / Aggie
Dustin / Dusty
Elvira / Vira
Matilda / Tilly, Matty
Lillian / Lilly, Lil
Barret / Barry, Bart

Shadrach / Shaddy
Nadine / Deeny, Naddy
Lambert / Bert, Bertie
Amanda / Mandy

Rebecca / Becky, Becka	Archibald / Archie
Macarthur / Mac	Barton / Bart
Sterling / Sterls	Dellereese / Della, Reesy
Emerald / Emmie	Elouise / Ellie, Veezy
Miriam / Mery	Daphne / Daff
Cinderella / Cindy, Ella	Basil / Bassy
Lawrence / Law, Larry	Barrington / Barry,Bart
Kenneth / Ken, Kenny, Kent	Eugene / Gene
Soloman / Solly	Eugenia / Gina, Genie
Monica / Mona, Nicka	Akeem / Keemy
Jackson / Jack, Jackie, Jacko	Beatrice / Bea
Jacob / Jake, Jakey	Gloria / Glo
Edward / Eddie, Ed	Candice / Candy
Jamal / Mally, Jay	Yvonne / Vonnie
Beverley / Bevs	Clothilda / Clothie, Lottie
Jasmin / Jazzy	Karen / Kay
Millicent / Millie	Gully / Godfrey
Evangeline / Vangy,Vanny	Beatrice / Bea

RANDOM NICKNAMES

Some nicknames were derived from random occurrences and personality and physical traits.

Many men who were known to have a strong Christian character would be referred to as 'Rev' by the people who knew them, even if they weren't actual preachers.

Sir T	Fergie	Ginger
Rollie	Biggie	Cookie
Tiger	Rev	Deac
Sarge	Cop	Soup
Letty	Shorty	Smitty
Froggy	Beanpole	Gussie Mae
Heads	Gippy	Sis
Doc	Cap	Teach
Bonnie	Scooter	Kempy
Mouse	Fish	Browny
Bro	Coops	Jonesy
Fatso	Sandsy	Ma lilly gal

MATCHING TWIN (BOY/GIRL) NAMES

As is the current practice everywhere, twins were given usually names that were similar. If not twins, these names could also be that of father and daughter. Below are some of the common names twins would be given:

<u>Boys Names / Girl's Names</u>

Adrian / Adrianne
Albert / Albertha, Abertina
Alexander / Alexandria
Alexis / Alexia
Alfred / Alfreda
Ambrose / Ambrosine
Andre / Andrea
Angelo / Angela, Agelina
Dennis / Denise
Donald / Donelle
Edwin / Edwina
Elvin / Elvina
Ernest / Ernestine
Eugene / Eugena, Eugenia
Francis / Francina, Francine
Frederick / Fredrica
Gabriel / Gabrielle
George / Georgette, Georgina
Gregory / Gregoria
Henry / Henrietta
Joseph / Josephine
Mark / Marsha
Michael / Michelle, Michaella

Anthony / Antonia, Antoinette
Austin / Austina
Cecil / Cecilene
Charles / Charlene
Charlton / Charlotte
Christopher / Christine
Clement / Clementine
Daniel / Danielle, Daniella
Nicholas / Nicolette
Oliver / Olivia, Olive
Patrick / Patricia
Paul / Paulette, Pauline
Phillip / Phillippa
Prince / Princess
Randolph / Randia, Randa
Ricardo / Ricardra
Robert / Robertha, Roberta
Samuel / Samantha
Stephen / Stephanie
Sylvan / Sylvia
Vernon / Veronica
Victor / Victoria
Virgil / Virginia

CHAPTER SIXTEEN

Foods We Love

Food creates a bond between Bahamian people; whether they are young or old, black or white, or from Nassau or one of the Family Islands.

Food was also a welcomed addition to any event be it a wedding, christening, engagement, marriage, ordinations promotion, retirement, graduation, birthday, anniversary, grand opening, seminar, setting up, funeral repass, baby shower, and bridal shower.

No matter the event, you got stuffed with food (stuff your gut), in fact, in many instances, these events were not deemed successful unless there was an abundance of the foods we love!!!

I recall when a family member was christened, we had arrived home to 'Keep up the Christening' (Continue the celebrations after the baby was prayed for and photos were taken).

After a while we noticed more than a few uninvited guests who enjoyed the food so much, they ate more than the invited guests, of course you know we were "up in arms about that", they ate more than the family and "tote" too.

Persons would look for parties just to enjoy the food.

As can be seen, food was an integral part of any event, and it was certainly a memorable part of my childhood. Some of our best family and church functions were centered around the abundance of good food.

The old folks would say, 'belly full, hind merry'.

LOCALLY GROWN FRUITS

In The Bahamas, we love sure love our fruits. The list below gives just a few fruits that we loved eating and all, if not many, of these were grown locally: -

Guanaberries	*White lady cocoa plum*
Guinep	*Star apple*
Bitter sweet orange	*Watermelon*
Plantain	*Almond (amond)*
Black lady cocoa plum	*Pigeon plum*
Custard apple	*Sugar apple*
Grapefruit	*Ju-ju*
Date palm fruit	*Peanuts*
Seagrape	*Darling plum*
Sour sop	*Red cherry*
Pineapple	*Guava*
Benny	*Mango / mangola*
Hog plum	*Avacardo pears*
Sugar cane	*Pomegranate*
Figs	*Paypaya (paw-paw)*
Coconuts	*Tamarind*
Scarlette plum	*Native bananas*
Governor plum	*Lime / lemon*
Sapodilla (dilly)	*Navel orange*
Tangerine	*Hog bananas*
Sugar bananas	*Star fruit*
Gooseberries	*Mammy saporter*
Mammy	*Mulberry*
Cantelope	*Jamaican apple*

LOCALLY GROWN VEGETABLES

The vegetables below have for many years been a staple part of Bahamian meals, and no Bahamian meal is complete without them:

Pigeon peas	Lima beans	Yam
Cassava	Guinea corn	Tomatoes
Onions	Finger pepper	Sweet pepper
Cucumber	Okra	Breadfruit
Green beans	Red beans	Eddy
Corn	Beets	Cabbage
Goat pepper	Bird pepper	Spice tree
Carrots	Spinach	Celery
Sweet potato	Chick peas	Spanish thyme
Thyme	Irish potato	Pumpkin
Rosemary	Cherry tomatoes	Lemon/lime

LOCAL TEAS

I recall as a young person; my mother would make different types of tea.

A very common tea was orange peel tea that was made by first pealing the orange peel off the orange and hanging it up to dry for about two weeks. Once it was dried, a piece of the dry peel would be boiled in hot water to make the tea.

There weren't many homes that you would enter without seeing orange peels hanging in the kitchen somewhere waiting for somebody to have delicious tasting orange peel tea eventually.

Here are some local teas that many, if not most persons, drank:

Pear leaf tea	Orange peel tea
Fever grass tea	Soursop leaf tea
Spice leaf tea	Sugar apple leaf tea
Mint leaf tea	Mango leaf tea
Lime / lemon leaf tea	Guava leaf tea
Dill seed tea	Cinnamon stick tea

a!-t

MRS TERRY ANN EVANS BAIN

MEDICINAL TEAS

As mentioned in Chapter 9, Bahamians have long been a fan if their "Bush Teas" or "Bush Medicine" and if you mentioned that something was hurting on you, rest assured a recommendation for some bush tea would follow.

Below are some of the common medicinal teas that were consumed:

Ceresee	Madeira bark (steeped)
Thyme tea	Aloes
Galawind (bruised and boiled)	Love vine (bruised and boiled)
Corn gruel	Jackmadar bush
Bajerine	Flour pap
5 finger bush (boiled)	21 gun salute
Pond bush	Castor oil leaf (bruised and boiled)
Shepherd needle	Ginger/nutmeg tea
Catnip tea	Pearoot tea

REFRESHING DRINKS

If you haven't noticed already, The Bahamas is hot! It was hot then as well. And when it was at its warmest, people always went for cold refreshing beverages. These are some of the beverages that were commonly consumed, particularly in hot humid weather.

Some of our favorites: -

Switcha (lemonade)	Cocoanut water (gully wash)
Strawberry soda with creme added	Malt tonic with creme added
Soursop and sweet milk drink	Mango juice

IF YOU HAVE A "SWEET MOUTH"

If you loved sweets and desserts, you'd be called a 'Sweet Mouth'. Or, it would be said that you had a 'Sweet Mouth.'

For all of you who are Sweet Mouths, here are some desserts we loved:

Peanut cake	*Coconut cake*
Pineapple jam	*Guava duff*
Light bread / rolls	*Bread pudding*
Banana pancake	*Cocoanut trifle*
Benny cake	*Creme cake*
Gooseberry jam	*Raison duff*
Johnny cake	*Banana pudding*
Cocoanut jimmy	*Warby*
Flour cake	*Pineapple tart*
Tamarind sauce	*Cassava bread*
Banana bread	*Raisin bread*
Guava cake	*Hot pepper jelly*
Cocoanut tart	*Guava jam*
Potato bread	*Raisin cake*
Corn bread	*Pound cake*
Fudge	*Pineapple upside down cake*
Gooseberry jam	*Soursop ice-cream*
Mango chutney	*Pineapple jam*

STORE   BOUGHT   SWEETS

Some of the popular treats that could be purchases at any store consisted of:

Long boy	*Cracker jack (in the box)*
Chocolate snaps	*Oh Henry*
Sugar daddy	*Bubble gum*
Sugar baby	*Snow cones*
Sugar mama	*Mounds*
Bounty	*Twinkies*
Whole nut	*Peanut butter*
Wrigleys gum	*Butterfinger*
Jello and Fruit cocktail	*Popsicles*

SOUPS, STEWS, SOUSES AND BOILS

No matter the weather, soups, stews, boils and souses were always a desired eat.

Bahamian men in my experience would eat these any time, even on Sundays which were usually reserved for the 'full spread'.

Dumpling soup is the preferred choice as it gives you a full feeling.

Here goes our soups:

Peas soup and dumpling	Bean soup
Mutton souse	Turkey souse
Hog gut souse (tripe)	Crab soup
Vegetable boil	Corn fritters
Split pea soup	Okra soup
Chicken souse	Pig feet souse
Crab and dough	Conch soup
Conch fritters	Seafood fritters
Conch stew	Turtle soup
Pig tail souse	Scorched conch
Pumpkin soup	Boil fish
Conch souse	Sheep tongue souse
Stew fish	Stuffed crab
Chicken foot souse (trotters)	Whelk souse

FOOD PREPARATION (setting your pot)

There were (and are) many ways to prepare the meats in the meal. All of the options below were used to prepare our favorite meats: -

Bake (conventional or rock oven)	Deep fat fry (cracked)
Smother	Scald off meat
Broil	Stew
Fry	Boil
Mince meat	Souse
Steam	Grill

YOU MUST HAVE YOUR SIDES

As is customary now, all meats were served with at least two side dishes. These were the common sides that accompanied the meats we had: -

Conch salad	*Potato salad*
Macaroni and cheese	*Roast corn*
Boil cabbage	*Mashed potatoes*
Seafood salad	*Lettuce and tomatoes*
Whelk salad	*Coleslaw*
Fried plantain	*Pickled beets*
Boil cassava	*Sweet peas*
Crab salad	*Candied yam*

RICE

No Bahamian meal is complete without rice – not now or then. And when you cooked rice, you had better get it right.

Family island cooks say that parboiled rice is a lazy way out. Very few households cooked white rice on Sunday, it was always a rice cooked with something.

These are the common rice combinations that were and still are eaten:

Peas and rice	*Kidney bean and rice*
Crab and rice	*Rice Bilao*
Vegetable rice	*White rice*
Black beans and rice	*Conch and rice*
Okra and rice	*Green lima bean and rice*
Corn and rice	*Rice cooked with lobster fat*
Black eye peas and rice	*Rice cooked with coconut milk/oil*
Pumpkin and rice	*Shrimp and rice*

YOU MUST HAVE YOUR RELISH (MEAT) TO GO ON TOP OF THE RICE

Just like in other places of the world, meat was the centerpiece of the meal and usually served on top of the rice.

The meat options below were (and still) commonly consumed items in Bahamian culture: -

Chicken	*Stew beef*
Stew beef	*Pork chops*
Pork chops	*Mackerel*
Mackerel	*Fish*
Fish	*Corn beef*
Corn beef	*Crawfish*
Crawfish	*Turtle*
Salmon	*Sardine*
Whelks	*Spareribs*
Steak	*Ham*
Hush-hush	*Lamb chops*
Hot dog	*Hamburger*
Conch	*Meatballs*
Tarpon	*Mutton*
Turkey	*Sausage*
Tuna	*Oxtail*
Liver	*Pot roast*

AND THEN THERE IS GRITS

In many instances, grits would take the place of rice.

Grits, which is a staple item in Bahamian breakfast, can also be prepared in a number of ways and served with different meats.

Here are some of the ways grits was prepared:

(Cooked with lard, wesson oil, crab fat or coconut oil or milk)

Peas and grits	*Conch and grits*
Corn and grits	*Crab and grits*
Bean and grits	*Okra and grits*

MEAT FROM THE SEA

We grew up loving and eating everything that came from the sea. I personally did not like turtle meat because when boiled, it produced a green jelly that was an acquired taste - I did not like it! I did, however, enjoy everything else on the list below: -

Red snapper	*Yellow tail*
Turbit	*Mutton*
Grunts	*Sea crab*
Barracuda	*Whelks*
Yellow snapper	*Broad shad*
Porgy	*Mutton snapper*
Logger head turtle	*Conch*
Shark	*Lionfish*
Goggle eye	*Tuna*
Grouper	*Hog fish*
Crawfish	*Jack*
Sting ray	*Sea crab*

ONLY IN THE BAHAMAS YOU KNOW THESE

Below are things that most Bahamians will recognize. They may or may not be found elsewhere, but we know and love these food items.

When somebody says they want some 'switcha', any Bahamian knows exactly what that is – lemonade.

When a Bahamian says they want some 'fire engine', we know they're referring to corned beef and white rice.

Gruel is cream of wheat with yellow cornmeal and was eaten primarily at breakfast time. And, how many people love their potcake?

Look at the list below and see how many of these foods you recognize and like: -

Gruel	Hush-hush
Smothered chicken	Dried conch
Tea and bread	Cups
Gully wash (unleaded cocoanut water)	Strawberry soda and creme added
Flour pap	Switcha
Horminy (grits)	Dried fish
Long water soup	Baggies
Trotters	Malt tonic and creme added
Potcake	Slam - bam
Scorch conch	Guinea corn grits
Salty sausage in bag with hot pepper sauce	Conch salad with mayonnaise added
Warby	Chicken-in-the-bag
Conch fritters	Crack conch
Fire engine	Long water soup
Porridge	Sweet milk and crème crackers

SPECIAL OCCASION MENUS

Of course, in The Bahamas, special holidays and occasions carried with them their own unique traditions. A large part of these traditions is the food that would be associated with that holiday. A great example of this is Good Friday, where Bahamians eat fried fish, peas and grits and hot cross buns. Full spread includes at least 3 meats, peas and rice, coleslaw, macaroni and cheese, potato salad, tossed salad, corn, beets, stuffing, fried plantain, peas soup and dumplings (optional), homemade rolls (optional), assorted soft drinks and of course switcha.

Below are a few holidays with the meals Bahamians normally have on these days: -

Good Fridays / You always ate fish with peas and grits, hot cross buns	*Post Watchnight Service / Fry fish, conch fritters, chicken souse, johnny cake*
Easter Sunday / FULL SPREAD	*Birthdays, Christenings, Showers & Graduations / Full Spread*
Mother's Day / Full Spread	*Wedding Reception / Full spread with all the trimmings*
Father's Day / Must have crab and rice	*Setting Up or Wakes / Souse, Johnny Cake, and Bush Teas*
Christmas Day / full spread with green peas and rice, ham and turkey	*Funeral Repass / FULL SPREAD*

BACK YARD FARMS

Every yard in the community, whether it be a street or corner, grew various crops; and when harvested, was shared among the neighbors.

Additionally, when the mailboat came in from the family islands, everyone would get a little parcel of "field produce" such as cassava, sweet potato, corn, eddie, pigeon peas, onions and cabbage.

These were always welcomed additions to the family pot.

Foods such as fish, conch, whelks crawfish and turtle meat were rare delicacies and were usually stored for special occasions.

Everyone seemed to have a "green thumb" or was said to have "a good hand for growing things."

The community back yard farms spanned over several yards, were seasonal and always had the following trees: -

MRS TERRY ANN EVANS BAIN

Hairy mangoes	Avacardo pears	Guava
Almond	Breadfruit	Ceresee
Dilly	Tamarind	Finger Pepper
Star apple	Peas	Gooseberries
Mangola	Cocoanuts	Aloes
Fig tree	Dill seed	Papaya
Canape	Goat pepper	Bird Pepper
Sea grape	Cocoa plums	Custard apple
Corn	Hog Plum	Mammy
Eddie	Scarlett Plum	Ju - Ju
Soursop	Sweet Potato	Sugarapple
Tomatoes	Cassava	Bajerine
Wild spinach	Lime / lemon tree	Mammy
(plentiful near the		Supporter
terlitts)		
Wild Thyme	Okra	Fever grass

Native Bananas   Guava Cake

Sapodillas

Traditional Bahamian Meal

Pineapples

CHAPTER SEVENTEEN

Pets

Every yard had a pet dog or cat that was treated like a member of the family. It seemed that boys usually liked dogs and the girls usually liked cats.

As far as we knew, there was only one breed of cats and two breeds of dogs - potcakes and German shepherds. Dogs protected the neighborhood and they barked fiercely at strangers and unfamiliar cars.

Dogs were given regular baths to avoid them getting the mange. They were usually fed every day from the leftovers of the family meal.

If the adults thought the pets had worms, they would give the animal catnip to eat which seemed to do the trick.

The biggest health threat to the dogs was "distemper" which seemed easy to catch and the dogs would often die. We grieved for our animals and gave them a decent yard burial.

Every dog and cat were given a pet name which they responded to very quickly after joining the family. Below are some of the given pet names.

COMMON DOG NAMES

Blackie	Binks	Caesar
Troy	Sheba	Abbey
Zoey	Muggy	Spotty
Scotty	Lion	Roger
Brownie	Bingo	Zeus

Rodman	*Bella*	*Butch*
Doodey	*Poonkey*	*Tiny*
Sammy	*Tiger*	*Sharkey*

COMMON CAT NAMES

Tabby	*Cupcake*	*Buttercup*
Kitty	*Dora*	*Nipsy*
Muffin	*Tom*	*Snowflake*
Marbles	*Fluffy*	*Feathers*
Angus	*Peaches*	*Cuddles*
Peebles		

Our Furry Friend

CHAPTER EIGHTEEN

School Days

School days were very structured even though the routine was the same. Each day began with a general assembly in the open courtyard for all students. There was Prayer, singing, a speaker on special occasions, and general announcements.

Students who excelled were applauded and, by the same token the ones who misbehaved were dealt with, sometimes publicly. Assemblies were quiet and orderly and on dismissal, each class walked in straight lines back to their classroom.

If the weather was bad assembly was held in the individual classrooms often shared by 2 teachers.

The headmaster made unannounced rounds during the day to most classes, often sitting in on a class for a while. Every headmaster I knew growing up was a firm disciplinarian, no-nonsense but humane.

Punishment was meted out on the spot or after school where you would collect books, clean the blackboard, and wipe down the desks. Prefects were not necessarily the smartest students but the better-behaved ones, they were chosen by the teacher.

The main purpose of a prefect was to assist with passing out and collecting papers, running small errands, and to 'call out the talkers' when the teacher had to leave the room, they kept order in the class. If the prefect misbehaved, he was stripped of the title and another appointed, to have this done was something you did not live down so easily. There was no detention or demerit system.

Just about everyone walked to school and you brought homemade lunch and your drink in a mayonnaise jar. Everyone wore uniform as we do now but skirts had to be knee length.

Having money was a rarity, only the well-to-do children were able to afford Clarke shoes from G. R. Sweeting, if your parents were able to "raise the wind" to get you one they were 2 sizes too big so that you don't outgrow them too soon.

When it rained you took off your shoes so they won't get wet or toejam will kill you the next day. You polished your shoes, did homework, and ironed your uniforms by Saturday with the Argo starch (a white powder mixed with warm water) then placed skirts under the mattress so that they can be stiff, you were not allowed to do them on Sunday, that was church all day.

During the 60's and 70's, the ministry had Truant Officers attached to the school system, there were only men officers who rode bicycles and small motorbikes.

They would visit the school regularly and get the names and addresses of the delinquent students, some of them we knew for sure played "hooky" or "played the trone".

It was a disgrace for one of them to come to your house, and, even worse if the parent was unaware that their child was "ducking " school. This was a major infraction on that child. Needless to say, this curbed a lot of truancy.

Homework was a must, heavy on the weekends. You were told the only excuses for not doing homework, your parents had to write a note, your house burned down, your house got flooded, your house had a break-in, you had a relative die and you were sick unto death.

Children would often be seen sitting on the field on Monday mornings trying to complete unfinished homework assignments.

In the last year of Primary school, all 6th-grade students had a general check-up from head to toe by the School Nurse.

Eye exams, teeth checked, and Booster Shots were given with the Parent's signed permission.

Mid-term breaks were introduced during the sixties, a welcome change to the term structure. Many "SPECIAL" days were celebrated during the school year besides Christmas, Easter, and Thanksgiving.

We celebrated "MAY DAY" where we planted the "MAYPOLE", "EMPIRE DAY", "THE QUEEN'S BIRTHDAY", field trips, and the "ANNUAL MUSIC FESTIVAL", usually held at Garfunkle Auditorium where schools showcased choirs, bands, choral speaking, and drama, it was always an exciting time.

The winning group was always given a special treat. We always looked forward to field trips, maybe twice in the school year. We were taken to historical sights, The Forts, The Water Tower, Blackbeards Tavern, The Airport, The Straw Market, Sir Harry Oakes Monument, Ardastra

Gardens and Jumbey Village. Jumbey Village was established by The Late Ed Moxey.

Each child was encouraged to give $2.00 to help with the building of that village. We all had a sense of pride when we visited because we felt as if we all helped to make history. The National Insurance Board now occupies that site.

The "COMMON ENTRANCE EXAM" was also started. It was a National exam offered to all 6th-grade students around the Bahamas in March or April of every year.

If you passed you were eligible to go to the Public or Private high school of your choice, and it was funded by the government. The successful candidates were announced on the Horace Wright show near the end of June. This was indeed a tense and exuberant time for parents as everyone gathered around their radios in anticipation of hearing their child's name. Cheers could be heard all over the neighbourhood as successful candidates were announced.

I passed the exam in 1969, a proud alumnus of William Gorgon Primary, and entered the illustrious halls of "THE GOVERNMENT HIGH SCHOOL".

Being the eldest of 8 children my Parents often said 'You set the pace'. Even though a public school it was the 1st choice for almost everyone.

We wore our royal blue jumpers and white blouses with pride and dared not sully the school's reputation by swearing, disorderly behavior or fighting in the streets, this could lead to suspension or in extreme cases expulsion.

We were unrivaled as we excelled academically and athletically, dominating both arenas. The GHS Country

Reigned. The curriculum was well-rounded and, encouraged students to become involved with the many clubs, such as Debate, Drama, Choir, Track and Field, Red Cross, Girl Guides, Rangers, Yearbook Committee, Christian Student Movement, and the Duke of Edinburgh Award Scheme, Boys Brigade, Boys Scouts, Girls Scouts, Girls Brigade, Path Finders, Drum and Bugle corps.

Just about everyone chose their LIFE professions in GHS and has excelled and stayed until retirement. I chose Nursing at that time

I graduated in 1974 a very proud Alumni of "THE GOVERMENT HIGH SCHOOL"

In 1975 I entered the Bahamas School of Nursing to become a registered nurse, graduating in 1979, and later as a midwife. I have worked in just about every Health Institution in the Bahamas, and nursed poor and wealthy, old and young.

My experiences as a nurse could be another book as it spans 43 years. I have seen the evolution of nursing in so many ways, some good others not as favourable.

Ms. Hilda Bowen the 1st Bahamian Matron was at the helm at the time of my formal training. She was very strict and had a no-nonsense policy. Pregnancy during our training was a no-no.

The hierarchy of respect was solid, you were not allowed to disobey orders and insubordination was frowned upon. A high standard of workmanship was expected at all times.

There were still a few English SISTERS around in 1975 but they were replaced by our Native daughters. I have spent 43 years in the Profession that I "LOVED", it brought me fulfillment and joy in serving my PROFESSION, my PEOPLE, my INSTITUTION, my COUNTRY, and "MY GOD".

It was a wonderful experience even with the hardships and the falls, but as a "LIFE PROFESSION" I would do it again in another life.

Nursing is a NOBLE profession, you not only give nursing care but your HEART to the persons you care for, the many VERBAL BLESSINGS that I have received from my patients over the years of my career have surely followed me.

I retired in 2018 with a grand farewell and a deep sense of pride and gratitude for a WONDERFUL CALLING.

School days were good days filled with fond memories of our favorite teachers and old friends, some of which became lifetime 'besties'. I clearly remember that we were told over and over again by our parents and teachers that a good sound education was the key to the world. What you truly learned could not be bought or taken away from you. In our parents' minds, 'Good learning' took three main forms. They were: -

1). School and book learning

2). Good home training based on the phrase - "Manners and respect take you through this world"

3). Church attendance and involvement

STRUCTURE

In the 1960's when I entered school for the first time, the education system was still under the Imperial regime.

The first classes were called the "PREP" schools. The Prep schools had class one and two.

You went to "JUNIOR" school next that went from Grade one to four. Next was the "SENIOR" school which went from fifth to the eighth grade.

PREP SCHOOLS

Eastern Prep #1 - Located on School Lane

Eastern Prep #2 - Now Speech Therapy Unit

Southern Prep #1 - Lodge Hall Building on Blue Hill Road and Fleming St.

Southern Prep #3 - now Stephen Dillet Primary School (both schools were in the same yard)

Southern Prep#2 - now Stephen Dillet Primary School

Western Prep #1 - on Quarry Mission Road

Western Prep #2 - now Woodcock Primary

Western Prep #3 - now Albury Sayles

JUNIOR SCHOOLS

Southern Junior School - now William Gordon Primary School

Western Junior School - now C. R. Walker School

Eastern Junior School - now Palmdale Primary School

SENIOR SCHOOLS

Southern Senior School - now A. F. Adderley High School

Western Senior School - now C. R. Walker High

Eastern Senior School - now Learning Resources Unit

TERTIARY EDUCATION

Bahamas Teachers College - now Eva Hilton Primary School

Hotel Training School - now C. C. Sweeting High School

Bahamas School of Nursing - Sands Lane

Nassau Technical College - now B. T.V.I.

Police College - Barracks on East Street

SPECIAL SCHOOLS

Stapleton School

The Centre for the DEAF

Salvation Army School for the BLIND.

TRADE SCHOOLS

Skinners Secretarial School

Sylvia Larrimore Crawford Sewing School

DRIVING SCHOOLS

Grants Driving School

Smith's Driving School

Adderley's Driving School

Maycock's Driving School

Quant's Driving School

LEGENDARY EDUCATORS

SCHOOLS NAMED AFTER THEM

There were many great educators that lived and existed in our time; and for many of them, their dedication was rewarded by having schools named after them.

The late Mrs. Anatol Rodgers to which a senior high school is named after was our high school principal at the Government High School during my attendance there.

The late Naomi Blatch who has a primary school bearing her name was a dear church member and my Sunday School Teacher when I attended Prep School where she was headmistress.

I am always very proud to say that I knew them personally.

Below is a list of many of our legendary educators:

A.F. Adderley High School
Clara Evans Primary School
Jack Haywood High School
S. C. Bootle High School
Albury - Sayles Primary School
Cleveland Eneas Primary School
James A. Pinder Primary School
S.C. McPherson High School
Andrea Archer Institute
Doris Johnson High School

Amy Roberts Primary School
D. W. Davis High School
L.W. Young High School
Sadie Curtis Primary School
Anatol Rodgers High School

D.W. Davis High School

Louise McDonald High School

Simpson Penn School
Thelma Gibson Primary School
C.I. Gibson High School

MRS TERRY ANN EVANS BAIN

Mable Walker Primary School
Stephen Dillet Primary School
B. A. Newton Primary School
E. P. Roberts Primary School
Majorie Davis Institute
Sybil Strachan Primary School
C.C. Sweeting High School
E.P. Roberts Primary School
Maurice Moore Primary School
T.A. Thompson Primary School
C.H. Reeves High School

Emma Cooper Primary School
N. G. M.. Major High School
R. N. Gomez All Age School
William Phipps Primary School
Carlton Francis Primary School
H. O. Nash Junior High School
R.M. Bailey High School

Erin Gilmore School
Naomi Blatch Primary School
Uriah McPhee Primary School
C.R. Walker High School
Eva Hilton Primary School
P. A. Gibson Primary School
Willard Patton Primary School
C.V. Bethel High School
Garvin Tynes Primary School

Preston Albury High School

William Gordon Primary School
C.W. Sawyer Primary School
Gerald Cash Primary School
Willimae Pratt School
Charles Saunders High School
Hugh Campbell Primary School
Keva Bethel
Dame Ivy Dumont

Brittany in primary
school (youngest
daughter)

Sebastian (school
days) in pre school

CHAPTER NINETEEN

Old Luxuries

With the size of our family, there were little to no extras for luxuries. This was very common. But despite this, our parents ensured that our needs were met.

Nothing was wasted or hardly ever thrown away as our parents would always make some use of everything. There was a high level of cleanliness and Saturdays were "scrub" days for cleaning the 'terlitt', clothes, house and the yard.

These chores were started early to free up your afternoons to go to the "show" (the movies) or other activities.

Do you remember these things and places that were our old luxuries?

HOW CAN YOU FORGET

Stroller shoes	Crendalin slip	Clapboard house
Jellosy window	Drop cord	Line stick
Thermos	Slop pail	Candle wick spread
Scratch broom	Florida water	Moroline
Robin or singlet	Figurines	Stucco house
Latch door	Clay pipe	Stenching stick
Slop bucket	Ice pick	Wicker furniture
Cush-cush perfume	Figurine stand	Vaseline
Pocket book	Panama hats	Wooden bucket
Window stick	Foam curlers	T.V. antenna
Iron bedstead	Grass mattress	Thrifty jitney
Fleishmans yeast	Spry or lard	Cloth pillow
Hair broaches	Collie pot	Moo-moo dress
Goose iron	Paper curlers	Straw fanner
Venetian blinds	Milk stands	Iron donkey
Royal crown	Rocking chair	Patch quilt
Catch a cowboy	Juke box	Bloomers

Smoothing iron	B.B. gun	Asthma powder
Lydia pinkam	Hot water bottle	The policy man
Clean off	Batten up	Coal stove
Record player	8 track tape	Belly band
Flour bag shirt	Razor strap	Search light
Smoking flax	Malt extract	Whomppers
On the throne	Chicken coop	Suspenders
Cassette tape	Whet stone	Flit
Drawers	Gentian violet	Stocking cap
Kerosene oil	Stockings	Rock oven
Crisco	Rubber pants	The ice man
Grater	Can cutter	Hair nets
Kerosene stove	The rent man	Eye glass
Buckleys white rub	Garter	Phensic tablets
Crab pen	Wash stand	Chewing tobacco
Birdseye diapers	Flit gun	Outside terlitt
Mercyrachome	Dutch oven	Shades
Carbolic soap, Lux, Lifebouy soap	Buckleys cough mixture	Wash (tin) tub
Argo starch in the box	House on four blocks	Smelling salts
Straightening comb / curler	Benjamin healing oil	Corsett (waist nipper)
Squashing out underwear	Hiding money in the block holes	Steel scrubbing pad
Keroene fridge	Phospherine, Buckfast, Wincarnis tonic wines	Long line girdle
Catching rain water in barrell	Airing out your clothes	Sanitary pads made of old rags
Brogue shoes	Barking almond	Limacol
House key under the mat	Penny, sixpence trupence, shilling, hapenny, pound notes	Money under the mattress
Wash\ scrubbing board	Putting ironed clothes under mattress	Mop made of rag cloths
House key over the door jam	Cartwright's garage	Tonka Tuff tennis
Huge satelitte dish	Rag in soda bottle for lamp (used in crabbing)	Sweet water black/white tennis
Kerosene lamp	Horse and buggy	Peblem Cloth
Economy jitney service	Big One Shoe store	Johnson's barber shop
Dawkins meat market	Nassau Glass	Keen Age dept. store

In Loving Memories barber shop	*Nassau Tile company*	*Moseley's Dry Goods store*
Economy hardware	*Dristan for the cold*	*Fox Hill Nursery*
Dorsette's hardware store	*Borden's Ice Cream company*	*Early Bird Supermarket*
Collie's barber shop	*Stop-n-shop*	*Hatchet Bay Plantation*

BOOKS EVERY HOUSE HAD

Bookcases were common in every household. Britannia Encyclopedias were a staple in most homes.

There was a man we affectionately named 'Uncle Binny' who would ride around on a bicycle selling the bedtime stories books and medical books to every house in the neighbourhood.

He would allow you to get books on a plan, the older folk called it 'paying it piecemeal'. We knew little about him but some people said he was a 7th Day.

When my granduncle came to town from Eleuthera we always looked forward to his story telling times, his memory was like a book.

My grandmother called them 'ole wives tales'. We thoroughly enjoyed his comical babookie and barabby stories and the scary tales of seeing 'spearits'.

He indeed was the life of the party.

Do you remember these books? Which of these did your family have?

Family Bible	*Tom sawyer*	*Uncle Arthur bedtime stories*
Church hymnal	*Bank book*	*On becoming a Woman*
Encyclopedia	*School texts books*	*Policy (insurance) books*

Royal readers	*Nancy Drew Novels*	*True romance magazines*
On becoming a Man	*Time Magazine*	*The Hardy boys*
Milo Butler exercise books	*Readers Digest*	*Uncle Tom's cabin*
Medical (doctor) books	*Jet/Ebony magazine*	*Funny (comic) books*
Mills and Boone	*National geographic magazine*	*Batelco phone book*
The Bobsy twins	*Tribune/Guardian*	*Our Daily Bread*

MUSICAL INSTRUMENTS

Musical instruments could be found in most homes. A popular pastime would be for the family to sing together while a family member played the guitar or piano.

In my home we had a piano and guitar; both of which my brothers and mother played very well. And who can forget Mommy's tambourine!

Most homes had one or more of the following musical instruments:

Foot pedal organ	*Banjo*
Saw and bow	*Tambourine*
Double rack hand clapping	*Goat skin drums*
Cowbells	*Piano*
Box guitar	*Good singing voices*
Tin tub, short pole, and fishing line	*Fiddle (violin)*
Whistles	*Shakers (dry pods of poincianna tree)*
Bugles	*Clackers*
Harmonica (mouth organ)	*Accordion (concertina)*

BAKERIES

For those of us who had 'sweet mouth' (See chapter 16), these bakeries below were some of our favorite places to go.

There was nothing better than going to Johnson bakery on Chapel Street on a Sunday night after church to get slice of freshly baked pound cake.

And who could forget Mrs. Conliffe's Bakery that supplied (and still does) birthday cakes and rolls for all our parties? There was no celebration without Mrs. Conliffe!

Which one of these bakeries was your favorite? What was your favorite item to get from there?

Paradise bakery	*Mrs. Conliffe Bakery*
Kelly bakery	*Purity bakery*
Swift Bakery	*Johnson Bakery*
Model bakery	*Community bakery*
Just rite bakery	

BANKS

There were very few banks for us to use then. My grandmother had a savings account at the post office up until she passed away.

In the family islands the post office bank was the only bank available for a long time.

Here are some of the banks we all used:

Royal Bank	*Bodie Bank*
Post Office Saving's Bank	*People's Penny Saving Bank*

POPULAR PHOTOGRAPHY STUDIOS

Before the rise in digital cameras and photography as we now know it, there were three main photography studios that everybody used to get their photos taken.

Sawyer's Studio was located on East Street. Capital Studios was located on Markct Street. Maxwell Studios was located in Dumping Ground Corner.

Wedding, christening, and all other photos were taken in the studio.

On the 1st Sunday of the month most babies were christened, so, you had to get to the studio early or anticipate a long wait.

The studios operated on a 1st come, 1st serve policy.

Our studios were:

Sawyers Studio	Capital Studios	Maxwell's Studio

PHARMACIES (DRUG STORES)

Here are a few of the pharmacies where we all went for our medicines, ointments and other related things.

The 'drug store' as we called it seemed to have everything you needed for any ailment you had. The pharmacist was put almost on the level as the doctor as they seemed so knowledgeable and informed.

It seemed as a child that they were never out of stock of anything.

There were only a few pharmacies:

Lowe's Pharmacy	Cole-Thompson Pharmacy
McCartney's Pharmacy	Tom - Mae's Pharmacy
City Pharmacy	

MRS TERRY ANN EVANS BAIN

YOU HAVE TO TRY THEIR FOOD

There were certain places that all Bahamians knew where to go to for good food. These places were not merely food establishments but cultural staples in the Bahamian community.

Who didn't go to Keith's for their famous chicken in the bag – especially late in the night? Who didn't go to Palm Tree for their big juicy burgers?

These places were not merely options, but places you had to go. Here they are:

Keith's	*Father Allen chicken shack*
Dirty's	*Howard Johnson restaurant*
Reef restaurant	*Johnson's in Chapel Street*
The Palm Tree	*The Shoal restaurant*
The big J	*3 Queen's restaurant*

ONE-OF-A-KIND STORES

These one-of-a-kind stores were scattered throughout Nassau the more well-known stores were on Bay Street.

When you heard your mother say she was going to "Town" that meant some heavy shopping on Bay Street.

If you were fortunate to accompany her you were intrigued by the sites and reasonable prices of the Ironmongery, Stop 'n Shop, and Jack 'n Jill.

We remember so well hopping on the Thrifty jitney, getting off the bus in front of the Nassau shop, and excitedly exploring most of the shops, it was a good but tiring day out.

Before getting back on the jitney for home you always got a hamburger from Burger House or a chicken snack from

130

Kentucky Fried Chicken (KFC). We looked forward to those days.

Here were the most popular stores during our days:

Madamoiselle
Central Furniture
Donld's furniture
The Nassau shop
Maura's
Butler's bargain mart
Bahamian lumber store
Fergie's food store
Atlantis satellite
Star insurance company
Mike's shoe store
Reuben's Variety Store
Williams Electric Store
Weeks bicycle shop
Melita's cloth store
Base Road Liqor Store
Heastie's Lumber and Building Supplies
Baker brothers
Bay Street Garage
Kelly's lumber yard
Wilson Shoe repair and sales shop
Mortimore's candy kitchen
Brice Garage
Thrifty hardware
Clarke's shoe store
Modernestic Dry Goods
The Jamaican Inn
House of sales
Maura's toy land
Horton's Bridal shop
Cavalier Construction
Russells dept store
Dorsette's food store
Young Miss Bridal Store
Kelly's
Christine and Johnny's
Carter record company
Bahamas supermarket
Nassau bicycle company
Robert's furniture

Bahamas Ironmongery store
Home furniture
Buck's record company
People's dry goods store
Higgs and Carroll satelite shop
Package delivery company
Christian book store
Alday's Variety Store
Hatchet Bay milk stands
Audley Kemp Liquor Store
Heastie's Paint
Hoffer and Sons
Williams bluefront store
Red Lion Bar
Jolly Roger's Paint
Stop and shop
Modernestic Garden and pet supplies
Bar 20
Jack and Jill
Pedican hat shop
The petty shops (in every community)
Portion control
City lumber yard
Rachel's boutique
Palmdale furniture
Deal's dept store
House of Value store
John Chea and sons food store
Symonettes 2nd hand furniture
Leo Carey food store
The linen shop
G. R., Sweeting dept store
Joy Martin shop
The Island shop
Sue nans
General hardware
Beneby's food store
The Blue Hill Golf Course
New Oriental Laundry
John Bull Store

131

MRS TERRY ANN EVANS BAIN

Malcolm's Garage	Jiffy Laundry Service
Cox food store	Fox Hill nursery
Lees carpet Craft	Gladstone Farms Ltd
Jolly Rodgers Paint	Deal's dept. store
Archers Nursery	Rocky farms
Hanna's Hardware	Thrifty Jitney service

GAS STATIONS

These were the gas stations everybody used. You learned as a driver to estimate your gauge properly and get to the station on time because most of them closed at 8pm at the latest.

If you ran out of gas after that time you had to stay put until the next day.

These were our stations:

Delaney gas station	Aranha gas station
Pickstock gas station	Mosely gas station
Ken Perigod gas station	Bahamas gas ltd.
Charles Moss gas ltd.	Heastie's gas station

WHICH ONE OF THEM SHOWS (MOVIE THEATER) YOU DOES GO TO

As a youngster, your reward for completing all of your chores (inclusive of doing homework, shining shoes, and ironing clothes) was a treat of a 4pm matinee at one of the movie theatres near you.

We always travelled in a group for safety. The group would pool our meager resources together to buy a big popcorn and drink to share between us. Everyone was able to get a pocketful of popcorn and a 'swig' of the drink.

These were really enjoyable and fun times and upon reflection left us with good memories.

The popular places to watch movies back then were:

Savoy Theater
Golden Gates Theater
Wulff Road Theater
Prince Charles Drive-in Theater
Cinema Theater
Capital Theater

Paul Meres Theater
Shirley Street Theater
Sunshine Twin Theater
Carmichael Drive-in Theater (now BFM)
Nassau Theater

POPULAR CLUBS - YOU JOIN ANY CLUB YET??

All of the clubs below except for the Red Cross and Crossroads were clubs that only the adults joined. Most adults joined some of these clubs as a status or social symbol.

Which of these clubs appealed to you:

The Mother's Club
Yellow Bird Club
Kiwanas
Anglican Church Men (A.C.M.)
Queen Mary Needlework Guild
The Lodge
Rotary
British Legion

Pilot Club
Burial Society
Toast Masters
Anglican Church Women (A.C.W.)
Lion's Club
Crossroads
Historical Society
The Red Cross

HOTELS (BIG AND SMALL)

Given that tourism is our biggest industry, we always had many hotels. And just like now, they were used for us to host our various events.

Sir Francis Hotel, for example, was a popular venue for wedding receptions. My wedding reception in 1983 was held at the Ambassador Beach Hotel.

Here are some of the popular hotels from back then:

Olive's Guest House
Emerald Beach Hotel
Nottage Guest House

133

Nassau Beach Hotel	*Ambassador Beach Hotel*	*Montague Beach Hotel*
Dolphin Hotel	*Marietta Hotel*	*The Corner Motel*
Rhinehart Hotel	*Poinciana Inn*	*Castaways Hotel*
Sheraton British Colonial Hotel	*Balmoral Beach Hotel*	*Sonesta Beach Hotel*
Crystal Palace	*Sir Francis Hotel*	*Anchorage Hotel*
Kentuckey springs Hotel	*Harbour Moon Hotel*	*Royal Victoria Hotel*
Towne Motel	*Breezes Hotel*	*Sandals hotel*
Grand Central Hotel		

There were other venues used for official social gatherings or important functions:

The Lion's Club	*The I.O.D.E. Hall*	*Wesley Methodist School Hall*
The House of Labour	*The Mother's Club*	*St. Matthews School Hall*
The Elks Rest	*Garfunkle Auditorium*	*The BPSU Hall*
The British Legion	*St. Agnes School Hall*	*The Dundus Civic Center*

POPULAR CLUBS AND BARS

Men were the most regular patrons at the bars and clubs, everyone had a favorite hangout spot during the week.

Weekends were dance and party times, at this time the women would join the men. Very few bars closed after 12 midnight, and, no bars were opened on Sundays and religious holidays.

Some bar owners sold their wares from their homes, they were known as "30 Days". If you were caught and prosecuted by the law you would face a fine and 30 Days in prison.

It was an "open secret" who did this, but, their customers did not rat them out because they would often say they were not going to "cut off their nose to spite their face". You were only able to buy cigars(King Edward), cigarettes(Salem, Camel, Winston), beers(Heineken, Becks, Budweiser, Guiness stout) and rum(Bacardi-rat bat, Gordons gin, Boones farm apple wine) from the bar. It was and still is illegal to sell these to minors.

Many performers in these clubs went on to attain worldwide fame.

Do you recall these clubs and bars:

Base road bar	Cat and the fiddle	Red Lion Bar club
Calypso club	Jungle club	Silver slipper club
The Junkanoo Club	The Zoo	Zanzibar club
Lover's holiday club	Fountain of Youth club	3 Queens restaurant and club
King and knights	Yellow bird club	Banana boat
Club waterloo	Peanuts Taylor	The Pink Slipper club
	Drumbeat club	

CAN YOU DANCE??

We Bahamians always loved to dance. Which one of these moves do you remember? Which one can you still do?

My older relatives all agree that they were the last generation that had good decent dance moves and good proper music.

My granduncle would always say their 'love music' was the real McCoy, not vulgar or too suggestive. He said that they were the real 'love gurus'.

Can you do any of these dance moves:

Rake and scrape	Mash potato
Wattozy	Twist
Funky chicken	Slow dance
Hokey - pokey	The stomp
Beat the conch style	Merangie
Quadril	Roach
The bump	The jig

The donkey | *Jumping dance*

ONLY A COUPLE OF UNDERTAKERS

When there was a death in the family, one of these gentlemen were usually called for the funeral and burial arrangements.

Most family islands had a Burial Society where you paid dues, this money was used to help with your funeral arrangements. Some enterprising islanders bought coffins which was given to the relatives of financial members.

This saved the family a lot of stress, money and headaches. If the member relocated to Nassau or any other island the coffin would be shipped there.

These were our Undertakers:

Pheally Demeritte | *Gerald Dean*
Boy Sweeting | *Marcus Bethel*

OUR MAIN DOCKS

Going to the dock with my grandmother to collect her box from Eleuthera from the mailboat was always exciting for me. Field produce and catches from the sea were neatly packed and taped up in boxes.

The meat boxes were stored in the boat's freezer. I listened with awe as the sailors would talk about the bad weather they encountered, and how they were able to 'fetch to land safely'.

I always thought to myself how brave and fearless these seamen were.

To this day I think that they are unsung heroes – possessing a skill and craft that has gone unrecognized for a long time.

The main docks were:

Prince George dock	*Arawak Cay*
Long Wharf	*Seabreeze canal*
Clifton Pier	*Coral Harbour canal*
South Beach canal	*Montague foreshore*
Potter's Cay dock	*South Beach ramp*

A DAY AT THE BEACH

You cannot think about fun without including beach days. We were always excited for certain holidays and events to pack up and go to the beach.

For example, our church's annual beach picnic, which for many years, was held at Yamacraw Beach. Aside from that, everybody could be found at the Long Wharf.

We grew up in South Beach, so, many days my mother and our next-door neighbour would make sandwiches from homemade bread and carry frozen switcha for a day at the beach.

We waited for the sun to go down to walk back home, we didn't risk getting more parched from the scorching sun.

Sometimes we fished for 'broad shads' and picked seagrapes when the season came. We cleaned our fish at the beach, they would be dinner the next day.

You slept like a log after a long day of romping and swimming in the sun. Beach time was always a happy time.

Favorite Beaches:

South Beach	*Montague Beach*
Adelaide Beach	*Rock Point*
Saunders Beach	*The Caves*
Goodman's Bay	*Jaws Beach*
Long Wharf	*Yamacraw Beach*
South Ocean Beach	*Clifton pier beach*

| *Delaport Point* | *Arawak cay* |
| *Coral harbour Beach* | *St. Andrews beach* |

GAMBLING

Bank then, Thursdays was race day at the Hobby Horse Race Track. Many people afterward would have to go home and do a lot of explaining.

Many light bills, house rent and grocery money was left at the track, after placing a sure bet on a horse.

Women were equally as guilty as men as participants in this vice. The closure of the track was met with much relief by many spouses and children.

Here are some of the popular gambling places and activities that people engaged in:

Percy Munnings	*Shoot dice*
Hobby Horse Race Track	*Shoot pool*
Shoot darts	*Play lottery*
Play Chicago	*Stokes Thompson*
Toote Numbers House	*Play cards*

THE MAILBOATS

Mailboats were usually the only means residents in the distant family islands were able to get supplies to them.

Depending on the weather, they would not see a mailboat for weeks. Those days had some hardship, but the family islanders had to make do.

Mailboat workers were very skilled sailors, and, without an official weather report, were able to recognize the signs that the weather was changing. This usually aided them in avoiding imminent danger.

Just as the mailboats were necessary, their names were very popular.

For example, the Yamacastle had a song written about it after it burned down in the 1960's.

Some of the well-known boats are listed below:

The Yamacastle	*The Acklins pride*
The Lisa J.	*The Captain Roberts*
The Mia dean	*The motor vessel Air Pheasant*
The Captain Sea	*Alice Mabel*
The Eleuthera express	*Gary Roberts*
The captain Dean	*Captain Moxey*

AIR TRAVEL

Air travel was considered a luxury, and there were not many airline companies.

Travel to the family islands was usually by helicopter or seaplane as most islands did not have proper airports or landing strips.

The only Bahamian airline during that time was called the Bahamas World Airline – which is now known as BahamasAir.

Below are the air carriers that serviced the Bahamas:

Pan-American Airways	*British Airways*
American Airlines	*Continental Airlines*
B.O.A.C.	*Air Canada*

PARKS

During the summer breaks our mothers often took us to a park nearby to "run off some of that energy".

The only main attraction was the swing, you had to stand in line to wait for your turn, but it was always enjoyable.

The only problem that arose was if somebody tried to jump the line before it was their turn.

The best-known parks were:

Southern recreation ground	*Carmichael Road park*
(Government Ground)	*(Bacardi Park)*
Windsor park	*Fox hill parade*
Christie park	*Highbury park*
Mason's addition park	*Malcolm park*
Chippingham Park	*R. M. Bailey Park*
Clifford park	*Freedom Farm*

NATIONAL EVENTS

We lived for National and Cultural events. Everything was an event

Our mother would dress me and my siblings up every year to watch the Labour Day parade (with umbrellas in tow).

While funerals were generally sad occasions, we definitely enjoyed the marching bands that would sometimes follow, especially at funerals on the family island.

One of the most anticipated events back then were the Church of God of Prophesy parades (Jumper Church March) that would start at the Church of God of Prophesy on East Street and end at the Western Esplanade.

Some of the other popular events were:

Fox hill day (planting maypole,	*Discovery day (Now National*
climbing greasy pole)	*Heroes Day)*
Police march	*Junkanoo parade*
Christmas carnival	*Crab fest*
Fishing tournaments	*Snapper tournament*
Labour day parade	*Patronal festivals*
Lodge marches	*Funeral marches*
National events at Clifford	*Homecomings (mainly family*
park	*islands)*
Pineapple Fest	*Independence Celebrations*

Bonefish Tournament	*Baptist day parade*
Jumper church march	*Youth marches*
The Red Cross Fair	*Regattas*
Trick or Treat	*Church fairs*

Coca Cola Bottles & Oil Lamp

Old Telephone

Goose Iron

CHAPTER TWENTY

Legends

The Bahamas has a rich and enviable history that every Bahamian should embrace and be proud of.

Records show that we can lift up our heads to the rising sun and proudly claim our heritage. I am saddened when I see my fellow countrymen walking, talking and dressing like people of a different country.

We have our own dialect (words and phrases only we understand), yet we are adopting other country's styles that are in many cases, substandard to our own unique culture.

We have so many songs, dances and stories that are quite colourful and are a true reflection of who we really are as Bahamian and sons and daughters of the soil.

So lift up your heads my people and be "black and proud".

RELIGIOUS LEADERS

Over the years, church has been and remains to be an integral part of our culture.

As such, many of the religious leaders have been well known and their names have become household names.

Who was inspired when hearing Rev. Charles Saunders preach (See Chapter 21)?

It should be noted that many of our preachers have achieved worldwide acclaim because of the competence and power with which they speak. Persons such as the late Myles Monroe, for instance, have made all Bahamians Proud.

The list of Bahamian religious leaders could be its own book, but here are a few of the more well-known leaders:

Elder W.H. Farrington	Pastor T. Michael Flowers	Evangelist Tom Roberts
Pastor Silas Mckinney	Rev. Timothy Stewart	Rev Leroy Roker
Rev. William Johnson	Rev. Arthur "Preacher" Rolle	Rev. William Makepeace
Rev. Michael Symonette	Rev. Charles W. Saunders	Father Marcian Peters
Rev. Alfred Nottage	Pastor Marcel Lightbourne	Evangelist Rex Major
Rev. H.W. Brown	Rev. O. A. Pratt	Rev. K.D. Josey
Rev. Eugene Patton	Rev. Edwin Taylor	Pastor A.H. Roach
Bishop Michael Eldon	Rev. Charles Thompson	Father Ettienne Bowleg
Bishop Alvin S. Moss	Rev. Kenris Taylor	Rev. Charles Sweeting
Rev. A, Samuel Colebrooke	Rev. Talmidge Sands	Rev. Harcourt Pinder
Bishop Drexal Gomez	Monsignor William Thompson	Bishop Brice Thompson
Rev. P.A. Gibson	Rev. K.S. Darling	Rev. Jeff Wood
Monsignor Preston Moss	Rev. Angela Palacious	Rev. Kenneth Huggins
Rev. W.G. Mcphee	Rev Charles Smith	Rev B.A. Newton

POLITICAL PIONEERS

Who can forget on July 10, 1973, when persons like myself went from being a British subject to a Bahamian citizen?

Our political leaders at that time were more than just politicians but in many cases were trailblazers in our eyes.

The main political parties during that time were:

The Progressive Liberal Party	The Worker's Party
The United Bahamian Party	The Free National Movement
The Bahamian Democratic Party	The Vanguard

Sir Lynden Pindling, for instance, is considered the father of the nation and the father of modern politics.

Here are a few well-known politicians:

Sir L.O. Pindling	Sir Randolph Fawes
Honorable Hubert ingraham	Sir Clement Maynard
Sir Arthur Foulkes	Honorable Norman Soloman
Honorable Kendall Nottage	Sir Gerald Cash
Honorable A.D. Hanna	Honorable Norman Soloman
Dame Margueriite Pindling	Sir Orville Turnquest
Sir Henry Taylor	Honorable Loftus Roker
Sir C.A. Smith	Sir Clifford Darling
Honorable Cadwell Armbrister	Honorable Shadrach Morris
Honorable Roland Symonette	Honorable Henry Bostwick
Honorable Paul Adderley	Sir Alvin Braynen
Honorable Ed Moxey	Dame Janet Bostwick
Dr. Norman Gay	Honorable Wilbert Moss
Sir Stafford Sands	Honorable Eddison Key
Honorable Bradley Roberts	Sir Milo Butler
Honorable Clarence Bain	Honorable Cynthia Pratt
Dame Ivy Dumont	Dr. Bernard Nottage
Dame Doris Johnson	Sir Randoll Fawkes
Sir Cecil Wallace-Whitfield	Honorable Shadrach Morris
Mr. C.A. Dorstte	Dame Janet Bostwick
Sir Kendal Isaacs	Honorable Cynthia Pratt
Dr. Norman Gay	Honorable Oscar Johnson

RADIO LEGENDS

In the days before television became wildly popular and accessible the radio was the prevailing source of entertainment.

Everyone tuned in at 1pm and 6pm to hear the news and death announcements. As children you did not disturb your parents or make a lot of noise at these times, they did not want to miss anything.

Messages were sent to alert a family member of sickness or to let them know to collect freight from the mailboat.

I remember going to the dock with my father who was sending food items to my grandparents in Andros. He would give the information to the dockmaster who assured that the message got to ZNS on time, then we rushed home to hear it on the news.

Who doesn't remember Rusty Bethel, who for a long time, was the voice of ZNS?

Who do you remember from this list?

Rusty Bethel	*Elva Russell*	*Phil Smith*
Ed Bethel	*Lionel Dorsette*	*Calsey Johnson*
Carl Pritchard	*Mike Smith*	*Carl Bethel*
Obie Wichcombe	*Cindy Williams*	*Jeff Scavella*
Charles Carter	*Steve Mckinney*	*Kirk Smith*
Nadine Campbell	*Bill Bain*	

LEGENDARY PROGRAMMES

I can recall on Wednesday evenings after the news that we'd sit and listen to 'The Fergusons of Farm Road'.

Miss Lye was the star of that programme, she would 'bust out' with a distinctive laugh that was loud and thunderous.

I think every Bahamian were sorely disappointed when the show came to an abrupt end.

That show provided us with many laughs and life lessons as it spoke to issues and common occurrences of the day.

Which of these shows was your favorite?

The Ferguson's of Farm Road	*Calypso Carnival*
Bon Airre	*Family Theatre*
Gospel Bells Programme	*Children Gospel Hour*
Aunt Annie and the Children	*Steve McKinney Show*
Voice of Prophecy	*Horace Wright Show*
Eventide	*Harvest Time*
Bert Cambridge Show	*The Charles Carter Show*
Saturday Night You Ask for it Show	*Gospel Song Time*

LEGENDARY ARTISTS

Bahamians are a talented people!

One of my favorite entertainers growing up was Pandora Gibson Gomez who was a comedian from Eleuthera.

She always told great clean jokes in her Eleuthera accent and had you rolling in the isles. And of course, we loved going to the Dundas Civic Center to watch one of James Catalin's many entertaining plays.

Who did you enjoy from this list when you were growing up?

Abigail Charlow	*Wendall Stuart*	*Jay Mitchell*
Timothy Gibson	*Bert Cambridge*	*Sweet Emily*
Alice Moncur	*Patricia Bazard*	*Gladston Adderley*
Ritchie Delamore	*Region Bells*	*Lou Adams*
Pat Carey	*Ed Moxey*	*Tony Seymour*
Cleophus Adderley	*Paul Meers*	*Maureen Duvalier*
Eddie Minnis	*Audrey Wright*	*Brad Lundy*
Tony McKay	*BBC Singers*	*Visionaires*
Nat Saunders	*George Symonette*	*Portia Carey*
Berkley Van Bird	*Ancient Man*	*Lee Callander*
Michael Maura	*Blind Blake*	*Nita Ellis*
Myron Walker	*Eloise Lewis*	*Dicey Doe Singers*
Joe Billy	*The Mighty makers*	*Joseph Spence*
Rebecca Chipman	*Monkey Man*	*Joanne Callender*
Mighty Sparrow	*Bro. George Barry*	*Clement Bethel*
Love Singers	*Terez Hepburn*	*Patricia Meicholas*
Priscilla Rollins	*James Catalin*	*Chippy Chipman*

Mark Gates Singers	Sir Sidney Poitier	Gayle Saunders
The Montague Three	Arthur Preacher Rolle	James Catalyn and Friends
Winston Saunders	The Blue Notes	Elon Moxey
Pandora Gibson Gomez	Ronny Butler and the Ramblers	Rev. Sammy Saunders
Charlie the yellow Bahamian	King Eric and his knights	Dr. Off (Tyrone Fritzgerald)
Golden Trumpeteers	Bahamas Brass Band	Lassie Doe and the boys
Amos Ferguson (Artist)	Ezra and the Polka Dots	Redemption Gospel Singers
Charlie Adamson	Count Bernadino	Clement Bethel
Beginning of the End	Sly and the Citations	Frankie Zharvargo Young
Sensational Sons of Joy	Redemption Gospel Singers	Leon Taylor and the Roosters
Freddie Munnings	Veronica Bishop	Visionaires
Piccalo the Preacher Man	Wilfred Solomon and the Magnetics	Kermit Ford (Leader of Drum and Bugle Corp)
Smokey 007	Sweet Exortist band	Pat Rahming
T. Connection	Peanuts Taylor	Dry Bread Group
Rachel Mackey	Andros Mighty Clouds of Joy	Ezra and the Polka Dots
Ishmael Lightbourne	Kayla Lockhart Edwards	Fireball Freddie the Magician

LEGENDARY ATHLETES

From time, our athletes have always excelled on the world stage.

Here's an interesting fact – Donald '9' Rolle, who was an excellent and accomplished golfer, lived only a few houses down from our family home.

Boston Blackie, who was a nice person to meet, was an accomplished boxer and definitely a local celebrity.

Here are several legendary athletes from back then:

Tommy Robinson	Tony Curry	Wenty Ford
Sugar Kid Bowe	Charlie Major	Betty Kenny
Ed Armbrister	Quincy Pratt	Freddie Higgs

148

Bobby Fernander	*Byron Musgrove*	*Austen Knowles*
Walter Callender	*Ray Minus Sr.*	*Ray Minus Jr.*
Andre Rodgers	*Hugh Bowleg*	*Elisha Obed*
Dr. Timothy	*Tom Grant (the*	*Mychal Thompson*
Barrette	*Bird)*	*(Sweet Bells)*
Boston Blackie	*Donald '9' Rolle*	*Phil Armbrister*
Andy Knowles	*Churchill Tenor*	*Leonard Dames*
	Knowles	*(Skeeter)*
John Antonas	*Sir Durwood*	*Mark Knowles*
	Knowles	

TRUE DOWN-HOME SONGS

Music is an integral part of our culture. There have been so many songs written and sung about our culture and reflect life as it truly exists.

One of my favorite local songs as a child was "Bahama Rock" by Ronnie Butler and the Ramblers.

Everything about it from the melody to the bass line moved me.

How many of these songs do you know? How many can you sing word for word?

Lassie sail ya boat	*You get swing*
Proud to be a Bahamian	*Watch the crab crawl*
Ask me why I run	*Got a letter from Miami*
Stop the world and let me off	*I'll get along somehow*
Miss Lye why you carry on so	*Sad to say I'm on my way*
Rat in da roof	*I'm a better woman than you*
Bain town millionaire	*Working for the yankee dollar*
Oh Liza see me here	*Let me se you raise your hand*
Sandra	*If I had the wings of a dove*
Tell me what more you want	*My son don't try to run -*
boy, ting a ling a ling	*shotgun wedding*
Pay me oh, pay me what you	*Do a nanny, do a nanny, how*
owe me	*ya do*
Up in the berry tree	*Mahalia where you been gal*
Ghost move	*Lemon tree very pretty*
Staggerlee	*Oh my Andros*
Diggin in ya bonegy	*Way down in Abaco*
My name is this, my name is	*Bad woman make good man*
that	*sleep in policeman hand*

149

MRS TERRY ANN EVANS BAIN

Nothing but a cuckoo soup
You never get a licking til you
go down to Bimini
Bush crack, man gone
You only know me when you
need me
Oh islands in da sun
Funky Nassau
Sail boat, sail boat, gat no
breeze to sail
Dance to the junkanoo
Mongo, mighty mongo
Did you see uncle Lou when he
fall in the well
Miss Lucy hang herself in the
mango tree
Islands in the stream
Talking fool is a very serious
thing
Damn fool ya married bagaulin

Exuma the obeah man
Jump in the line, rock ya body
on time
Shut ya mouth go away, mama
looka boo-boo day
Turn around and let me see
Ma Ma bake the johnny cake
Christmas coming
Gimme my shirt, gimme my
tings
Angelina
Mama lay, lay, lay
Get involved

Mammy no light in the kitchen
Eleuthera- oh lidy die, oh lidy
die die oh
All day all night Miss Maryann
I am dancing with Vernita
Daylight come and she want to
go home
Oh Sam oh Sam, oh Sam no
good Sam
I'll try anything once
Straighten up and fly right
Wake up early one morning
kiss my mama goodbye

Something just ain't right
Everybody want to go to
heaven but nobody wan dead
Inagua is the best kept secret
Who the cap fits let them wear
it
I sorry for you boy
Ya born here, ya born here
Going to Cat Island, join the
rake n scrape band
Conch ain gat no bone
Naughty Johnny
Mama don't like no rakin and
scrappin in here
Wine daddy wine, shake Lucy
shake
Try and try again boy
Tell ole lying him he better
come down
They comin by boat, dey comin
by plane
Oh my commanding wife
Every married man got his on
bonefish
We rushig, we rushing, we
rushing through the crowd
Will you still love me tomorrow
Whoa is me, shame and
scandal in the family
Yellow bird, up high in banana
tree
If the cap fits let them wear it
Gal tell me who do you love
If ya Mah send you to school
you better go
Dogs don't bark at parked cars
If my galfriend leave me I ain
ga cry
Centipede knock to ma dollar
I'm your private dancer
Come back liza come back girl,
wipe the tears from me eyes
Who put the pepper in the
Vaseline
Bring back the good ole days
Going down Burma road
If I give you some of this thing
you ga talk it

150

When Bain town woman catch
a fire, even the devil run
Emily you make me crazy
Matilda
Gin and cocoanut water
Blame it on the water
My birthday come again
Pretty blue eyes do come out
tonight

Bahama rock
Age ain't nuttin but a number

If you touch that thing ya
mama ga know
Give me some sweet potato
bread
Church out, crab crawling
When I die bury me deep
Brownskin gal stay home and
mind baby
Nearly married da gaulin

Junkanoo in ya belly,
junkanoo in ya soul
Hice up the jumbee sail
Loose me let me go
Island woman
Party in da backyard
All night and day I thinking
bout you
Don't rock the boat baby
No young gal ga make me a
slave
Melody amour
Can't find Jerry Roker in town

Mama come here quick bring
me that licking stick
Gal if I had you
The cure for the cuckoo soup
Nosy mother-in-law
Independence morning
Bonefish Foley
My mama told me 3 years ago,
I must'nt marry no drunken
man
You got the best of my love
If the Good Lord never went on
Holiday
Mamma don't want no peas
and rice and coconut oil
Don't know what it is the
monkey wan do
Living the life of a single man
Sponger Money
Jones oh Jones you can't last
long
Sly mongoose dog know your
name
My name is Morgan but it ain't
J. P.
Send them home
Coconut water
Delia gone
Angelina
Went on the bay one morning
met Mr. Cooper crying
Working for the yankee dollar
Tell me dat again boy

OH my commanding wife
Roach on my bread

CHAPTER TWENTY-ONE

What Church House Ya Go To?

G rowing up every one had a church affiliation for "just in case ", you need something to fall back on for important times. The late Great Preacher and Educator, Rev. Dr. Charles W. Saunders said it so eloquently years ago, that people use church for the 3 main areas of their lives, when they HATCH, MATCH and DISPATCH.

HATCH - When the babies are Christened

MATCH - When you get married

DISPATCH - For funerals

DENOMINATIONS

If there is one thing The Bahamas has plenty of, its churches. Back then, churches came under one of the below denomination groups.

While each denomination had its own proper name, many had nicknames that are still used today. For example, the Church of God of Prophecy churches were referred to as 'Jumper Churches' because of their lively style of worship and interaction during their services – which included a lot of jumping.

Here are the church denominations that existed at that time:

Catholic - Carclick	*Church Of God - Josey Church*
Jehovah's Witness (J.W.'S)	*Methodist*
Church Of God/ 7th Day	*Holiness*

Assembly Of God	*Baptist*
Anglican	*Presbyterian*
Pentecostal	*Haitian Baptist*
Church Of God Inc.	*Lutheran*
Full Gospel	*Church Of Christ*
Seventh Day Adventist - 7th Day	*Church Of God Of Prophecy*
	(Prophecy Church, Jumper
	Church)
African Methodist Episcopal	*Brethren - Gospel Hall, Hold The*
(A.M.E.)	*Right*

Most Catholic and Anglican Churches have Rectories; The Catholic nuns were housed at St Martin's Convent and the Monks at St. Augustine's Monastery.

Most family Island Churches had Mission Houses

FAMILIAR PHRASES ASSOCIATED WITH CHURCH

Anybody who was involved in church and/or regularly attended church would know that church had it own set of phrases and jargon that was used.

If somebody was said to have "fallen from grace" or "backslide", you know that their faith was in question or that they were living lives inconsistent with the faith.

If somebody attended a 'jumper church', the liveliness of their services was usually described as a 'hand clapping, foot stomping' time.

How many of the phrases below do you remember? How many of these do we still use?

Lay hands on	*Baptismal classes*
I all Prayed up	*Run scriptures*
Sacraments or the Lord's Supper	*Preach up a storm*
High mass	*He's a high member*
Anoint with olive oil	*Membership class*
Take right hand of fellowship	*Full of learning*
Pick up an error spirit	*Sing up a breeze*
Long dress and rough dry hair	*Say recitations*
Run song service	*Heaven help us*

Bring heaven down
Under the spirit
Lead song time
Fall from grace
Pray the heaven open
Give out tracts
Preach his head off
Backslide
March my foot off
Glorified dust
Speak in tongues
Hey GLORY
Sing my head off
Gone to the bench
Run testimony service
Heavenly minded, no earthly good
Need to repent in sack cloth and ashes
God always has the last say
Preach fire and brimstone message
Saved, Sanctified and filled with the Holy Ghost
Moving of the spirit
Lord have mercy on his poor soul
Hand clapping, foot stomping
Put on your shouting shoes
He hold a high billet in church
Let everything that hath breath, PRAISE THE LORD
God ain't no poppy show
Rev mash some corns today
It;s a good thing God ain't like man
Prayer line
Gone on a mission
Confessional on Saturday evening

Say grace
Leading of the spirit
GLORY TO GOD
He miss his calling
Take up collection
Deeper sink for a higher rise
THANK YOU JESUS
Street meeting
Church rally
Concert prayer
Setting up
Visitation
Have the spirit
Sing out
He left some big shoes to fill
It's the gospel truth
I never see him darken the doors of the church in my life
Mouth fulla God
Rush out
Family that prays together, stays together
He musse christmas, not Christian
Let go and let God
Choir practice
Take up a purse for them
He in church but ain nuttin to him
You need to say 10 Hail Mary's for that
You need to go to Confession
Its a good thing GOD aint like man
Beyond a shadow of a doubt
Great God Almighty what a time
He lose his way
GOD moves in mysterious ways

OFFICIAL TITLES OF THE CLERGY

If you had a leadership position in church, one of the titles below would usually prefix your name.

Many high-ranking leaders were very protective of their "title", so you were very careful to address them properly, risking the fate of a public and embarrassing rebuke. If you were an emcee, you paid close attention to details such as

154

these. Here are the titles that many of the church leaders would have:

Bishop	*Priest*	*Elder*
Lay reader	*Justice of the peace*	*Prophet*
Arch deacon	*Catechist*	*Chief Apostle*
Sexton	*Superintendent*	*Ambassador*
Pastor	*Minister*	*Leader*
Lay preacher	*Marriage officer*	*Apostle*
Disciple	*Arch Bishop*	*Prelate*
Youth Minister	*Deacon*	*His Grace*
Presiding Bishop /	*Evangelist*	*The Very Reverend*
Elder		
Deaconess	*Proselyte*	*Chairman*
Overseer	*First Lady*	*Associate Pastor*

OTHER CHURCH OFFICERS

Even if you were not a church leader with a title, everybody still had a role in their church.

Prayer Band Leaders would normally go to the church two or three times per week at 5:00 am and have prayer meetings. They were affectionately referred to as the bedrock of the church.

To be a Prayer Band Leader was a position that carried much respect, most Prayer leaders could bring Heaven down with their Prayers!

Which of these roles did you fulfill? Do you still do it now?

Church Secretary	*Church Cleaner*
Altar boys	*Sextons*
Choir, soloists, worship leaders	*Sunday School Teachers*
Visitation Team	*Choir Master*
Church Bell Ringer	*Peoples Warden*
Sound room technicians	*Musicians*
Prayer Band leaders	*Men's / Women's Fellowship*
Bible Study Leader	*Altar Guild*
Pulpit Ministers	*Mission Team*
Ushers	*Parking lot attendant*

DRESS CODE

When going to church on Saturday or Sunday there was a church dress code and cardinal rules everyone adhered to no matter what denomination you belonged to.

Below are some of the rules that the different churches enforced:

The Jumpers, 7th Day and Holiness women didn't comb press their hair, wear pants at any time or wore makeup or jewelry.
No women wore pants to church.
Most women wore hats or chapel caps to church.

You always sat with your parents or a relative.

You did not chew gum in church.
Easter colours were pink, baby blue yellow or lime green. You wore a bonnet, lacy gloves and hanky and frilly socks. A heart shaped straw hand fan was fashionable.

Dresses were not fitted and they were knee length'
Men always wore full suits to church.
Women with newborns did not come to church until the baby was christened.
Special dress up days were Easter and Christmas.
You did not write in the church hymn books.

At Christmas you wore shades of green, red and brown.
Straight black was always worn to funerals.
Women usually wore all white on Palm Sunday and Mother's Day or Women's Day
All white was also worn at Baptisms and Confirmations
Choir robes were prized possessions and many persons often desired to be interred in them

OLD TIME SINGS

As young children we were taken on street meetings and Prayer meetings on a regular basis.

It was during this time we learned so many beautiful songs of the Faith that seem to be disappearing from memory.

This segment is meant to recapture the essence of the "old time sings"

God is still on the throne
The Holy Ghost power
Good time up in heaven
I love the Lord

When He calls me
I know it was the blood
The preaching of the gospel
(traditional)
Don't turn back (traditional)
I Am Delivered
The lord will make a way
Gimme dat Old time religion
Thank you Jesus
If you live right
Bound for The kingdom
He lifted me up
He never failed me yet
He brought me out from the miry clay

I'm so glad Jesus lifted me
Everywhere He went
Was out on the rolling sea
I'm going home on the Morning train
Glory, glory, Hallelujah
David's harp (traditional)
It will soon be done

Somebody touched me
Lord oh Lord (traditional)
Something in my heart
It's me oh lord
Roll, Jordan, roll
My Lord is sweet
We going to a meeting
Up above my head
What you think about Jesus
The Lord is good, good

SPECIAL CHURCH CELEBRATIONS/SERVICES

No matter what church you belong to there was always some special celebrations throughout the year, almost every month.

The church calendar was full. I grew up in the Gospel Hall church and the highlight for us as children was the annual Sunday School Prizegiving usually held either just before Easter or Christmas.

Each class recited, sang or did a short skit to the delight and cheers of parents and visitors. The climax of the night was each child was given a gift and a bag of goodies.

Outstanding students were also rewarded for good attendance and scripture memorization.

The evening usually held on a Friday was a much anticipated event for us growing up in church.

157

Here are some of the 'Special Days' of the church year:

Church anniversary	Patronal march
Convocation	Confession
Watch night rush out	Women's day
Christmas carol service	Singspiration
Pastor's anniversary	Mothering Sunday
Revival services	Mother's Day
Youth day	Men's day
Concert	Pentecost Sunday
Evensong	Deliverance service
Father's Day	Receiving into Membership Sunday
Usher's day	Choir day/choir practice
General assembly	Prayer meeting
Consecration service	Tarrying service
Church anniversary	Baptism
Prayer band day	Children's day
Missionary circle	Bible study
Lent	Christening
Prize giving	Women's fellowship
Easter	Wedding
Pastor appreciation day	Youth guild
Good Friday	Funeral
Synod	Men's Fellowship
Whit Sunday	Christmas
Conclave	Church business meeting
Confirmation	Advent season
Missionary Sunday	Special 'call meeting'
Convention	Sunday school day
Cantata	Holy week
Conference	Watch night service
Crusades	Special week of Prayer

FUNDRAISING

There's a myriad of activities in any church that require some fundraising. There is a running joke that every church has a building fund that lasts for years.

If you were a regular church goer, or even if you weren't a regular church goer, you know about one or more of these fundraising activities:

Building fund	Mission fund	Bake sale
Bingo night	Benevolent fund	Bus fund

Jumble sale	*Special envelopes*	*Cook out*
Fair / bazaar	*Pledges*	*Gospel concerts*

*Gospel concerts: if concert held in church, offering taken up after a hot number, or money placed on podium during a rousing song, or money pinned on a singer by excited audience

POPULAR OL' TIME GOSPEL GROUPS AND SINGERS

One of our favorite pastimes on a Sunday night after church was attending Gospel concerts.

A lot of them were held at the S. C. McPherson School, which was a central location at that time.

Admission to those events were usually $3.00, so we saved up especially for these times, The concerts were always enjoyable and inspirational and got to enjoy a bevy of our local artists.

These were the show stoppers of the Gospel arena:

Alice Moncur	*Region Bells*	*Dicey Doe Singers*
Golden Trumpeteers	*Sammy Saunders*	*Gospel Bells Choir*
Love Singers	*Dioscison Chorale*	*Dr. J. J. Barry*
Mark Gates and the	*Andros Mighty Clouds*	*Sensational Sons of*
Temple Time Singers	*of Joy*	*Joy*
Kayla Lockhart	*Arthur (Preacher)*	*Redemption Gospel*
Edwards	*Rolle*	*Singers*
Joseph Spence	*Ismael Lightbourne*	*Rahming Brothers*
Cooling Waters	*Visionaires*	*Preston Wallace*
Pratt Brothers	*Simeon Outten*	*Tabernacle Concert*
		Choir
Errol Rolle	*Rachel Mackey*	*Myron Walker*
Gladstone Adderley	*BBC Singers*	*Bro. George Barry*
Simeon Outten	*The Gospel Pearls*	*Sweet Revival*
Gospel Impressions	*Cooling Waters*	Mark Gates Quartet

MRS TERRY ANN EVANS BAIN

DO YOU REMEMBER THESE RADIO PROGRAMMES?

As televisions in the home were not common as they are now, the radio was a great source of entertainment. There were several religious radio shows that we loved to listen to at home, especially in the evening time.

Which one was your favorite?

Bonaire radio	*Eventide*
Gospel Song Time	*Voice of Prophecy Programme*
Dr. J. Vernon McGhee	*Family Heartbeat Theatre*
Faith Temple Song Time	*Aunt Annie and the Children*
Billy Graham	*Harvest Time*
Burt Cambridge Show	*Aunt Mae and the Children*
Rev. Buddy Tucker	*Morning Devotions*
Praise Ye The Lord	*Live Church Service Broadcast*

OL' TIME SINGS

When the saints	*I got a robe*
Revival in my soul	*Starry crown (traditional)*
God's heaven is so high	*My Lord's a writing*
Lay down my burden	*God is good*
Something got a hold on me	*God never fails*
Look where God has brought us	Come Peter row your boat
Going down Jordon	*Learning to lean on Jesus*
Lead me and guide me	*God is so good*
Thank God I'm free	Go Mary tell my Disciples

GRAVEYARDS/CEMETARIES

Growing up, there were only a few public graveyards around. In this era, most, if not all, funerals took place on Sundays. And how can we forget, funerals usually had a marching band (especially on the islands).

It's funny to think about now, but back then as children, we were afraid to walk past cemeteries, particularly in the night times – less a 'spearit' come and take you away or follow you home.

160

There were both public and private church cemeteries. Here are the cemeteries that were around then.

PUBLIC CEMETERIES

Western cemetery
Marshall View cemetery
Infant View cemetery
Fox Hill cemetery
R.A.F. cemetery - for War Veterans

Old Trail Cemetery
Adelaide cemetery
Eastern Cemetery
Gambier cemetery

PRIVATE CHURCH CEMETERIES

Most, if not all, Family Island churches have their own graveyard next to, or in a very close proximity, to the church. I once attended a funeral for a close family member in Eleuthera, and the graveyard was just about 200 yards away.

When the funeral had ended, we marched around an area called the "coppit" before going to the gravesite.

In Nassau if the graveyard is next to the church, there would be a march from the funeral home or from the longest road nearest to the church.

Nassau churches that have adjoining or very nearby cemeteries:

Ebenezer Methodist Church
St. Joseph's Catholic Church
St. Matthews Anglican Church
St. Bede's Catholic Church
St. John's Baptist Church
Sacred Heart Catholic Church
Bethel Baptist Church
Mount Carey Baptist Church
St. Agnes Anglican Church
St. Ann's Anglican Church
Wesley Methodist Church
The Catholic Cemetery

St. Mary's Anglican Church
St. Mark's Baptist Church
Coke Methodist Church
St. Paul's Baptist Church(Fox Hill)
Macedonia Baptist Church
St. Augustine's cemetery
St. James Baptist Church
St. Margaret's cemetery
St. Barnabus Anglican Church
St. James Anglican Church
St. Anselams Catholic Church
St. Peter's Baptist Church - Gambier Village

OLD TIME SINGS (PART 3)

Every time I feel the spirit, moving in my heart I will pray
By and by
The last mile of the way.
Swing low, sweet chariot
If you never needed the Lord
When He calls me

Somebody needs you Lord

Can't nobody do me like Jesus
Said I wasn't gonna tell nobody
Meeting tonight
Yes God is real
I love the Lord

LAST RITES

Having your relative die was very difficult and stressful, especially on the family islands for so many reasons. There was very limited communication as phones were very scarce. Only a very few of the islands had an airport, they relied mainly on the mailboats, and, they could not sail if the "weather was kickin up".

No island had a morgue or a funeral home, so, bodies could not be kept for more than 24 hours. If a person is sick and seems to be "getting low" relatives try to get "word" to the ones in Nassau by telegraph so they can come or take them to Nassau before they "cross over".

The nurse or police wire the information into Nassau after the person dies then things move swiftly after that. Sadly because of these serious lacks many, many deaths and funerals were missed, we have come a long way.

The dead person is laid on the floor of their home and wrapped in a white sheet. Their face is tied up and a bowl of coarse salt is placed on their stomach to keep it from swelling up. In the hot summer, the sheet is kept wet until burial.

Most people were buried in their Lodge apparel or church robes, they often wrote out their service and will before they passed away. The carpenter of the community measures and builds the coffin covering it with a nice sheet or candlewick spread.

The mason of the settlement would ensure the grave is dug and curbed out; he later makes a headstone. The coffin spray is made up of local flowers.

The dressed deceased is laid out in his living room or parlor until funeral time. Meanwhile, the women are busy cooking up something for after the service.

If the family was able to get the person to Nassau before they died and their wishes were for an island burial, then things were slightly different. The corpse would go down on the boat and laid out for a day in the family home.

A "wake" or "setting up" would be held the night before the funeral. It would start about eight'ish and go until 4am in the morning. It was conducted by the elder people of the settlement.

They brought out all the songbooks and took turns calling out the hymns and saying if they were long or short meter. Different persons would sing a solo or give short reflections of the dear departed. You were kept awake by constant rounds of souse, johnny cake and bush teas. Around 3-4 the Pastor would give a short word so the crowd could disperse and "ketch yasef" before the funeral

There was a procession from home to the church.

Growing up everyone knew a 'professional mourner' who went to every funeral and screamed and hollered for the deceased even if they were their 25th cousin.

If closely related they would 'root bout' the place often losing a watch, or an earring, dirtying their clothes, mashing up a hat, or losing a foot of shoe. Sometimes they would try to jump into the open grave, but put-up little resistance when restrained.

The coffin is tightly shut at the church, everyone walks to the graveyard with local band music. Most churches in the islands had a graveyard adjacent to the church so you would march around "the coppit" (street in area of church) in a final tribute.

If someone in the community had a truck or buggy it served as a hearse. The community cemeteries were always by the sea and were always well-kept. Nobody walked past graveyards at night for fear of "spirits following you home".

If you had to pass one you repeated "ten, ten, the Bible ten" the whole time to ward off the "spearits".

Burial societies were formed in most islands to assist during the time of death as there was no insurances. In recent years they have been purchasing coffins and making them available to it's members.

The treasurer of the society takes an active role in not only collecting dues,but issuing funds and ensuring that the whole process goes well.

Most people would talk to the Pastor or Priest before "crossing over", making many death bed confessions cause "they don't want to die with anything on their chest".

WILLS are usually read at the cemetery or a short time later, often a source of confusion and grief. The wills when written are witnessed by the Clergy, the Police or the Island Commissioner or the Nurse.

A lot of families were left "COMMONAGE PROPERTY". Anyone born into the family line or their descendants has a rite to a parcel of land in that area.

The Administrator is appointed by the senior family members and can be removed or challenged if found to be unethical or unfair. This property cannot be sold or leased.

Following the funeral townsfolk would visit grieving persons regularly; bringing food to make sure they keep your mind together.

AFTER FUNERAL TALKS

No funeral experience was complete without the 'after funeral talks'. After funeral talks could take place a few days or weeks after a funeral. When this took place, relatives and others would sit around and discuss all that happened before, during and after the funeral – referred to figuratively as a "postmortem".

When people partook in the after-funeral talks, this is what you were most likely hear:

Chile dey couldn't be comforted	*She hard boy*
I feel so sorry for dat poor womam / man	*I know he turning over in his grave when he see how things turned out*
Everybody was feelin it for her	*Dey was passing out and fluttering like chickens*
He ain leave them a single thing	*I know she coming back to hag them*
Only those who knows it, feels it	*She couldn't ketch hersef*
I hear he leave them fixed	*She was so wretched, I hope she resting in Peace*
Alla them break down from the start	*Dey root bout and holler all over the ground*

MRS TERRY ANN EVANS BAIN

I hear he leave dem straight
I hear he ain leave them a dime

He sign everything over to his
brother
She had to bury him outta her
pocket
He ain had nothing

I hope she don't die from fretation
Dey bury him like a pauper

He pray for her to die
She / he ain gat nobody left in
this world
He ga fret hesef right out this world
Trust me, she better off without
him
Dey didn't do right by her / him
after all he do for them
She was so sick we thought we was
ga bury her first
I hope dere conscience lickin dem
Ain't the sickest go the quickest
She / he outta all dere suffering

For how sick he was he last long

She ga pine all away
I surprise she last so long

All the fun done

Boy, death is one thing you don't
plan for
You never miss the water
He drop down dead so fast

I hear dey spending all his hard
earned money
He plan he own funeral
Dey spending his money like dirt

What a time eh?

Dey even ain wait til the dust clears

I still in shock bout the whole thing

Death don't care who he take
She tried to drop in the hole, I
woulda let her
If it was for money he woulda still
been here
She was letting out some piercing
screams
If life was a thing that money could
buy
I ain like how he look
I hope the Lord have mercy on his
soul
He did look dead
He straight, you ain gatta worry
bout where he gone
She did look like she was sleeping
He was all dey depended on

I hear dey carry on bad

Death is no respect of persons

Everybody put him right in heaven
Chile, live you may, die you must
Chile I didn't know that person they
was talking bout in that coffin
You ain bring nothing jn this world
and you can't carry nothing out
I know he bust hell wide open
I hear most alla dem in their family
die from the same ting
That was a special death that get
him
They treat him so bad I hope he
pull their big toe
I hear she/he die bad
She ga take a while before she get
over this
I hear she talk all her deeds on her
deathbed
I hope he make it in
I thought they was gonna put him
down better than that
Only God one know when God and
man reconcile
She was dressed like she looking
out
Well she had enough time to repent

166

She cry like her heart was broken

Dat's a serious blow

*Dey was dropping down like flies
all over the place*
Chile I hope she recover from this
Dey holler the place down
She was outta it the whole time

Dey sure tear down the place
*I hear he plan and write out
everything before he die*
She ain shed a tear

*She ain worry but nuttin, dey ga
bury me for stinkness or sweetness*

*I hear he sweetheart was there
hollering too*
*There wasn't nuttin he wouldn't do
for them*
*I don't think he ga last 6 months
before he married*
I hear they turn their back on him
He used to lead a double life
*He pour every dime he had into
them children, and for them to
treat him like that*
I hear he had 2 families
That's the least they could do

*Where all dem chirren come from
hollering "Daddy"*
Lord have mercy on his soul

Emmanuel Gospel Chapel
Nassau, Bahamas

CHAPTER TWENTY-TWO

What Island You Hail From?

I t was not unusual when adults met each other for the first time, after the initial introduction, the first thing they wanted to know is - what island you hail from and who are your peoples dem.

Eleutherians, Harbour Islanders and Spanish wells descendants had a dialect that set them apart, they sound a little like native Americans but they seemed to add an "H" to every word.

Acklins and Crooked Islanders also had a distinct tone almost slurring their words. Cat Islanders tended to hold onto their words long with a dragging accent. Turks Islanders sound like low-key Americans.

So, your dialect and manner of speaking gave you away. Next certain surnames were usually associated with different islands

Family Islands - all of the townships are made up of "settlements", each settlement had a name and had these attached to it :- Sound, Point, Cay, Town, Bay, Creek, Hill, Pines, Haven, Field, Bluff, Rock, Harbour, Coppit, Bight, Cistern, Bogue, Tract, End, Bush, Ground, Ville, Cape.

New Providence the capital on the other had;- Parks, Way, Alley, Avenue, Corner, Estates, Land, Road, Street,

Boulevard, Crescent, Terrace, Highway, Close, Gardens, Hills, Heights, Town, Addition, Village, Drive, Dale, Ville, Ridge.

The Bahamas also has many attractions that are wonders of the world: Blue Holes, Ocean Holes, Starfish drop, Glass Window Bridge, Queen's Staircase, Water tower, Lighthouses, Garden of the Groves, Salt Ponds, Swimming Pigs, Flamingoes, Iguanas, Wild donkeys, Pink Sand, Mount Vernon, Fort Charlotte, Fort Montague, Fort Nassau, Gestapo Grotto, Columbus Landing Point, Sir Harry Oakes Monument, Queen Victoria Statue, Columbus Statue, Black Beard's Tower

We will now visit each island, their settlements and surnames most common to that island.

ABACO

CAPITAL : Marsh Harbour

Most Abaconians were fishermen, farmers and sailors. the famous 'Dean' line of boaters that ran mailboats hailed from Sandy Point. The women are good cooks and bakers and are very skilled in needlework crafts.

SETTLEMENTS:- Cedar Harbour, Dundas Town, Crossing Rocks, Pelican Shores, Mount Hope, Fox Town, Central Pines, Spanish Cay, Moore's Island, Crown Haven, Grand Cay, Little Orchard, Joe's Creek, Wood Cay, Elbow Cay, Hope Town, Spring City, Marsh Harbour, Murphy Town, Cooper's Town, Green Turtle Cay, Treasure Cay, Sandy Point, Man o War Cay, Blackwood, Cherokee Sound, The Mud, Pigeon Pea,

170

Sand Bank, Cassurina Point, Great Guana Cay, Yellow Pine, Smith's Hill.

SURNAMES :- Albury, Archer, Sawyer, Bain, Bethel, Bootle, Bowe, Clarke, Collins, Cornish, Curry, Dames, Davis, Dawkins, Douglas, Edgecombe, Eldon, Fox, Heild, Higgs, Key, Lowe, Malone, McBride, McIntosh, Knowles, Mills, Parker, Pinder, Innis, Reckley, Roberts, Pritchard, Russell, Campbell, Sweeting, Weatherford, Murray, Williams, Wilmore, Ingraham, Hunt, Minns.

ACKLINS

One of the most southerly islanders has a reputation of having some of the most resilient people, they have known many hardships over the years so they can pinch a penny. They are Farmers, fishermen and recently the export of sisal has become one of their main trades.

SETTLEMENTS :- Lovely Bay, Delectable Bay, Hard Hill, Selena Point, Chesters, Mason's Bay, Spring Point, Pinefield.

SURNAMES :- Tynes, Heastie, Hanna, Beneby, Ferguson, Cox, Bain, Collie, Emmanuel, Deveaux, Darling, Johnson, Moss, Pearson, Roker, Williamson.

ANDROS

CAPITAL : Nicholls Town (North); Fresh Creek (Central); Kemp's Bay (South)

Andros also known as the big yard is the largest island in the Bahamas. Sailor's, boat builders, spongers, farmers, crab catching, forestry, bone fishing are but a few of the regular crafts done by Androsians. Wild hogs, blue holes and tales of the Chicharney is also a trademark of Andros.

SETTLEMENTS :- San Andros, Red Bays, Nicholls Town, Conch Sound, Lowe Sound, Morgans Bluff, Barc Community, Blanket Sound, Calabash Bay, Fresh Creek, Love Hill, Miller's Hill, Small Hope Bay, Mastic Point, Stafford Creek, Staniard Creek, Mars Bay, Behring Point, Bowen Sound, Mano War Sound, Burnt Rock, Cargill Creek, Grant's Hill, Orange Hill, Lisbon Creek, Little Harbour, Pinders, Swains, Bastian Point, Congo Town, Driggs Hill, Deep Creek, Black Point, Pure Gold, Duncombe Coppit, Ferguson's, High Rock, Kemp's Bay, Little Creek, Smith's Hill, The Bluff, Buzzard Bay.

SURNAMES :- Adderley, Andrews, Bain, Barr, Bastian, Bell, Bethel, Bowleg, Boyles, Braynen, Brown, Bullard, Burrows, Canter, Campbell, Christie, Clarke, Claire, Coakley, Colebrooke, Davis, Duncombe, Evans, Flowers, Forbes, Fowler, Gaitor, Gray, Gibson, Grant, Green, Hanna, Hendfield, Hinsey, Hutcheson, Johnson, Kemp, Knowles , Lightbourne, Mackey, Marshall, Martin, McKenzie, McNeil, McPhee, Miller, Minnis, Moxey, Minns, Moxey, Nairn, Newton, Neely, Neymour, Oliver, Pickstock, Porter, Pratt, Rahming, Riley, Roberts, Rolle, Russell, Sands, Saunders, Scott, Stuart, Thompson, Walkes, Wallace, Williams, Wilson, Wright, Woods, Woodside, Sumner, McGregor, Peet, Lundy, Bell, Balfour, Wilkerson, Romer, Coleby, Foulkes, Minus, Moultrie, Pennerman

BERRY ISLANDS

CAPITAL : Bullocks Harbour

One of our smallest communities that has fishing as one of it's main line of work.

SETTLEMENTS :- Great Harbour Cay, Bullocks Harbour, Shark Creek.

SURNAMES :- Gomez, Francis, Winder, Brennen, Simmons, Kerr

BIMINI

CAPITAL : Alice Town

Made up of 2 small islands, north and south Bimini, with the north island being more populated. They connect using a ferry boat several times a day. Diving and fishing are their main tourists attractions.

SETTLEMENTS :- Alice Town, Porgy Bay, Bailey Town, Cat Cay, Bucaneer Point, Port Royal.

SURNAMES :- Weech, Sherman, Robins, Saunders, Ellis, Francis, Brown, Stuart, Levarity, Roberts, Pinder, Rolle.

CAT ISLAND

CAPITAL : Arthur's Town

Cat Island the birthplace of Sir. Sidney Poitier are a people proud of their heritage. Humble beginnings with large families, they made their livelihood through farming, salt mining and . straw-work products. Cat Island has also been renown for producing a large number of distinguished educators. It is also the home of Rake-N-Scrape.

SETTLEMENTS :- Old Bight, New Bight, Hawkes Nest, Smith's Bay, Port Howe, Arthur's Town, The Bluff, Orange Creek, Pigeon Cay, McQueens, Devils Point, Baintown, Flamingo Bay, Tea Bay, Bahama Sound, Bennetts Harbour, Shanna Bay, Dumfries, Steventon, Zonicle Hill, The Cove, Wilson Bay, Industrious Hill, Knowles, Rokers, Moss Town.

SURNAMES :- Armbrister, Bain, Bonamy, Burrows, Bonaby, Romer, Campbell, Cleare, Dean, Dorsette, Gilbert, Hepburn, King, Johnson, Marshall, Moncur, Newbold, Poitier, Rolle, Seymour, Stewart, Stubbs, Adderley, Thurston, Turner, Strachan, Davis, Mackey, Flowers, Roach, McKenzie, Larrimore, McMinns, Dawkins, Zonicle, Jackson, Evans, Josey, Strapp, Pratt

CROOKED ISLAND

CAPITAL : Colonel Hill

Crooked Island is one of the most southerly islands located nearby Acklins. Their population is not very large and fishing and farming is their main source of income along with sisal exports products. Like Acklins they have experienced many hardships over the years and are able to make a dollar stretch.

SETTLEMENTS :- Cabbage Hill, Colonel Hill, Richmond, Majors Cay, Fairfield, Cripple Hill, Landreal Point, Church Grove, Pittstown Point, Long Cay, True Blue.

174

SURNAMES :- Anderson, Rose, Cunningham, Miller, Scavella, Bonaby, Daxon, Deleveaux, Farquason, Simms, Laroda.

ELEUTHERA

CAPITAL : Governor's Harbour

Eleuthera known as the land of freedom is home to the famous ocean hole, the Preacher's Cave, the glass window bridge and the pineapple fruit, which has made Hawaii popular. It was once the home of the Levy plant which employed many Bahamians, who produced high quality dairy products. Many silos can be seen throughout the island. Many residents still do farming and fishing for a living. Mr. Timothy Gibson an outstanding educator hailed from Savannah Sound and is the composer of our national anthem. Eleuthera has many teachers whose schools bear their names, C.W. Sawyer, Thelma Gibson and C.I. Gibson.

SETTLEMENTS :- Cupids Cay, The Bluff, Blackwood, Whale Point, Current Island, Lower Bogue, Upper Bogue, Gregory Town, Hatchet Bay, James Cistern, Governors Harbour, North Palmetto Point, South Palmetto Point, Savannah Sound, Windermere Island, Tarpum Bay, Rock Sound, Winding Bay, Green Castle, John Millers, Deep Creek, Whymms Bight, Waterford, Bannerman Town, Lighthouse Point.

SURNAMES :- Adair, Albury, Allan, Anderson, Bethell, Blatch, Brown, Bullard, Burrows, Carey, Cambridge, Cash, Cates, Clarke, Cleare, Cooper, Culmer, Curry,

Davis, Edwards, Gibson, Goodman, Grant, Griffin, Hall, Hilton, Hudson, Hunt, Ingraham, Johnson, Kemp, Knowles, Leary, Mackey, Major, McCartney, McHardy, McKinney, Meadows, Mingo, Moree, Miller, Moss, Neely, Newbold, Nixon, Pedican, Petty, Pinder, Pyfrom, Rankine, Richards, Sawyer, Rolle, Sands, Scavella, Smith, Stuart, Sweeting, Symonette, Thompson, Morris, Williams, Morley, Young, Whymms, Jolly, Strachan, Fisher, Elliott, Ward, Cumberbatch, Silos (North Eleuthera).

EXUMA AND THE EXUMA CAYS

CAPITAL : George Town

Made up of over 100 cays Exuma has become the tourism mecca, offering attractions as Starfish Drop, The Swimming Pigs, Gestapo Grotto, Pink Sand and the ever popular Exuma regattas which draws large crowds. On a clear day cay hopping and sight seeing is a tourists dream. Farming and fishing has now been replaced with employment at the award winning Emerald Bay hotel which boasts of high occupancy almost year round.

SETTLEMENTS :- Duck Bay, Stocking Island, Elizabeth Island, Gunana Cay, Fowl Cay, Crab Cay, Hog Cay, Moriah Harbour Cay, Glass Cay, Black Cay(Black Point), Soldier Cay, Perpalls Cay, Green Turtle Cay, Davy Cay, Tommy Youngs Cay, Culmers Cay, Bonefish Cay, Channel Cays, Jewfish Cay, Bowe Cay, Coakley Cay, Square Rock, Farmers Cay, Staniel Cay, Rat Cay, Bob Cay, Manowar Cay, Normans Cay, Hawsbill Cay, Sampson Cay, Green Guana Cay, Brigertine Cays, Harts,

Barretarre, Rolleville, Alexander, Steventon, Harry Cay, Flamingo Bay, Richmond Hill, Emerald Bay, Farmers Hill, Forest, Mount Thompson, Ramseys, Moss Town, The Bluff, Hoopers Bay, Tar Bay, Georgetown, Rokers Point, Rolletown, Hartswell, Ferry, Forbes Hill, West Palm Beach, Williams Town, Stuart Manor, Curtis, Sandy Point, Anns Tract, Hermitage, Calvin Hill, Pigeon Cay.

SURNAMES :- Bannister, Bodie, Bowe, Bullard, Clarke, Cooper, Curry, Curtis, Dames, Davis, Dorsette, Ferguson, Gray, Johnson, Knowles, Lloyd, McKenzie, Minns, Morley, Munroe, Musgrove, Patton Roach, Rolle, Sears, Smith, Storr, Williams, Ramsey

GRAND BAHAMA

CAPITAL : West End

The second largest populated island of the Bahamas, and the city of Freeport is run by the Port Authority. The garden of the groves is one of its main attractons. Efforts are being made to revitalize its once booming hotel industry.It also is the only other island that offers comprehensive health care opportunities, and, extensive radio and television services. University and Police trainings are also held here. Syntex, Borco and the Container Port provide a large number of Grand Bahamians with lucrative employment.

SETTLEMENTS :- West End, Holmes Rock, Eight Mile Rock, Bartlette Town, Hepburn Town, Pinders Point, Hunters, Freeport, Lucaya, Mather Town, Freetown, Bevans Town, High Rock, Pelican Point, Rocky Creek, McClains Town, August Cay, Harbour Cay, Deep Water

Cay, Sweetings Cay, Lightbournes Cay, Michaels Cay, Long Cay, Crab Cay, Man-o-war Cay, Little Water Cay.

SURNAMES :- Aranha, Baillou, Bartlette, Beckles, Been, Bevans, Bridgewater, Cooper, DeGregory, Delancey, Duncombe, Edden, Edwards, Farrington, Forbes, Fox, Franks, Gardner, Gilbert, Grant, Green, Hall, Hamilton, Hendfield, Hepburn, Heild, Higgs, Hunt, Jennings, Johnson, Jones, Kemp, Knowles, Laing, Lewis, Lightbourne, Lopez, Mallory, Marshall, Martin, McAlpine, McClain, McDonald, McIntosh, McKenzie, McPhee, Miller, Missick, Moore, Mullings, Munnings, Murray, Nesbitt, Neymour, Outten, Newman, Parker, Pintard, Pratt, Pritchards, Rigby, Richards, Roberts, Robinson, Rolle, Rose, Russell, Saunders, Seymour, Shepherd, Simmons, Smith, Strachan, Stubbs, Stirrup, Swann, Sweeting, Swain, Taylor, Tate, Thompson, Walker, Walkine, Watson, Wildgoose, Williams, Young, Wilchcombe, Levarity, Russell, Perpall.

HARBOUR ISLAND

Harbour Island is one of the smallest islands of the Bahamas. In recent years it has become one of the major tourists attractions for tourists and natives alike. The pink sand is its selling feature. The day away trip is the activity of choice.

CAPITAL: Dunmore Town

SURNAMES :- Percentie, Barry, Higgs, Saunders, Grant, Johnson, Sawyer, Mingo, Roberts, Mather, Albury.

INAGUA

CAPITAL : Matthew Town

Inagua is said to be the best kept secret in the Bahamas. Home of the Protected flamingoes where thosands live, and of course a vibrant wild donkey population. There is an historic light house, a Defense Force base and the Morton salt company that hire 80% of the islands populas. Employment here affords them a reasonably high standard of living.

SETTLEMENTS :- Matthew Town, Lake Windsor, Light House Point.

SURNAMES :- Franks, Ford, Palacious, Fawkes, Symonette, Farquason, Allen, Cartwright, Cox, Seymour, McIntosh, Mullings, Nixon, Pickering, Moultrie, Benjamin, Hanna, Granger

LONG CAY

CAPITAL : Albert Town

A small sparsely populated cay next to Acklins and Crooked Island. Main source of income is fishing.

SETTLEMENT :- Albert Town

SURNAMES :- Farquason.

LONG ISLAND

CAPITAL : Clarence Town

MRS TERRY ANN EVANS BAIN

Situated in the north west Bahamas, it was given its name because of its length. A resilient and proud people they have made their mark as A-1 boatsmen, winning many national races. They have also set themselves apart as goat farmers, salt refiners and fruit and vegetable farmers. Most of the women are good straw craft producers. The high light of the year is the annual regatta which attracts boat enthusiasts from all over.

SETTLEMENTS :- Berrys, North End, Seymours, Cape Santa Maria, Burnt Ground, Stella Marris, O'neils, Simms, Wemyss, Millers, McCanns, Thompson Bay, Salt Pond, Indian Hole Point, Pinders, The Bight, Grays, Deadmans Cay, Buckleys, Cartwrights, Pettys, Hamilton, Scrub Hill, Deans, Clarence Town, Dunmores, Morrisville, Hard Bargain, Cabbage Point, Mortimors, Gordons, South End, Cape verde, Deals.

SURNAMES :- Adderley, Burrows, Carroll, Cartwright, Constantakis, Darville, Deal, Dean, Fox, Gibson, Gray, Harding, Knowles, Major, Martinborough, McCardy, McHardy, Miller, Moree, Mortimore, Pinder, Pratt, Rigby, Ritchie, Rolle, Shearer, Simms, Smith, Taylor, Treco, Turnquest, Wallace, Watson, Wells, Newchurch, Morris, Simmons, Whylly

MAYAGUANA

CAPITAL : Betsy Bay

A small island set far away from the others. Fishing and boating their main form of income. Mayguana has produced some of the largest conchs. recently it becoming a popular tourist attraction offering rest, relaxation in simple

180

form while enjoying its nature beauty and inviting beaches. Most Mayguanians excell academically and do very well in the job market.

SETTLEMENTS :- Abrahams Bay, Pirates Well, Betsy Bay.

SURNAMES :- Charlton, Brooks, Brown, Deveaux, Deleveaux, Hamilton, Bain, Higgins, Nesbitt, Williamson, Murphy, Black, Collie, McPhee, Farrington, McFall

RAGGED ISLAND

CAPITAL : Duncan Town

Ragged Island also one of our far away sparsely populated islands. Some of the biggest fishes and conchs also come from here. Most of the native are fair to look at, beautiful women, handsome men with skin as indian hue. Fishing and salt mining is their main livelihood. Efforts are being made to restore the infrastructure of the island which was exensively damaged during a hurricane a few years ago.

SETTLEMENTS :- Duncan Town

SURNAMES :- Lockhart, Munroe, Wilson, Wallace, Walkine, Maycock, Curling, Moxey.

RUM CAY

CAPITAL : Port Nelson

A small island nestled next to San Salvador. It has a population of less than 200. They have a vibrant population of wild goats and most men fish for a living. Beautiful and set apart the natives live a peaceful serene life.

SETTLEMENT :- Port Nelson

SURNAMES :- Strachan, Douglas, Bain, Butler, Farrington.

SAN SALVADOR

CAPITAL : Cockburn Town

San Salvador is one of the diving capitals of the world, its deep blue clear waters are a divers dream. It was one of the first to have a Club Med. In the sixties and early seventies it housed the Bahamas Teachers College and a Naval Base. Fishing and farming was the mainstay of the islanders . One of the main attractions is Columbus Landing where Columbus made his stop. It also houses one of the oldest light house in the country.

SETTLEMENTS :- Cockburn Town, United Estates, Halls Landing, North Victoria Hill, South Victoria Hill, Sugar Loaf, Long Bay, Sandy Point, Columbus Landing.

SURNAMES :- Lightfoot, Fernander, Butler, Clarke, Jones, Edgecombe, Forbes, Arnette, Douglas, Nairn, Storr.

SPANISH WELLS

Spanish Wells is a quaint village nestled between Eleuthera and Harbour Island. They have done well in their main industry of fishing which has afforded them a comfortable way of life and earned them the title of the fishing capital of the Bahamas. Spanish Wells natives take great pride in their community, it is always clean and well kept. The men are well known fishermen who go out for weeks at a time, they have made a decent living from the export of their catches. The women are very good bakers and produce very beautiful needle work products. The health care facility is state of the art and they boast of being one of the first family islands to have their own morgue.

SETTLEMENT :- St. Georges Cay

SURNAMES :- Neilly, Lowe, Malone, Pinder, Albury, Curry, Higgs, Russell, Sawyer, Sweeting, Perry, Underwood.

TURKS AND CAICOS ISLANDS

CAPITAL : Providentiales

Once considered part of the Bahamas, these natives make up a big part of our population. The Turks like the Bahamas has many islands and Cays seperated by large bodies of water and accessable by boats and planes. They remain under British jurisdiction and are a part of the Commonwealth of Nations as we are. They enjoy close ties with the Bahamas and are assisted when necessary. Like the Bahamas one of their main source of income is fishing and most recently have enhanced their tourist appeal.

SETTLEMENTS :- Providentialles, North Caicos, Middle Caicos, South Caicos, Grand Turk, Salt Cay, Parrot Cay, Pine Cay, Ambergris Cay, West Caicos, Littlle Water Cay, East Caicos.

SURNAMES :- Hendfield, Hall, Walkine, Missick, Gardner, Spencer, Lightbourne, Ewing, Bain, Forbes, Cox, Delaney, Delancey, Capron, Swann, Reckley, Astwood, Hamilton, Malcolm, Lotmore, Grant, Phillips, Moore, Robinson, Quant, Mills, Levarity, Butterfield, Hanchell, Gibbs, Duncanson, Scriven, Outten, Simmons, Swain.

NEW PROVIDENCE

CAPITAL : Nassau

New Providence is the capital, one of the smaller islands and the most densely populated. All major polilitical, social, religeous and secular activities are held here. More schools are in one constituency that is in a whole family island. The Governors, Prime Minister, training colleges and major institutions are held here in the capital, which makes it very busy indeed.

SUBDIVISIONS :- In Nassau the townships are called subdivisions and not settlements. There are so many, Heights, Hills, Beach, Town, Gardens, Village, Estates, Road, Streets.

Fox Hill, Fort Hill, Chippingham, Pyfroms Addition, Adelaide, The Grove, Gambier, Bainstown, Grantstown, Culmersville, Yellow Elder Gardens, Garden Hills, South Beach Estates, Elizabeth Estates, Stapledon Gardens, Black Village, Big Pond, Montell Heights, Englerston, Marathon, Highbury Park, Bamboo Town, Jones Heights, Seabreeze Estates, Blue Hills Estates, Bozine Town, Millenium Gardens, Munson Village, Centerville, Freetown, Blair Estates, Garden View Estates, Monastery Park, Johson

Road Subdivision, Winton Meadows, Little Hyde Park, Sandilands Village, Yamacraw Beach Estates, Eastwood Estates, Eastern Estates, Camperdown, Foxdale, Redland Acres, Nassau Village, Sea Beach Estates, Albany, Mount Pleasant Green, Tusculum, Lyford Cay, Westridge, Millers Heights, Gamble Heights, Coral Harbour, Joans Heights, Pinewood Gardens, Dignity Gardens, Englerston, Ridgeland Park, Faith Gardens, Belair Estates, Masons Addition, Oakes Field, Prospect Ridge, Delaport, Sandyport, Charlotteville, Imperial Park, Malcolm Allotment, Kennedy Subdivision, Penny bank Subdivision, Shirley Heights, Peardale, Pinedale , Rockcrusher Subdivision, The Grove-Bay Street, Majors Subdivision, Five Pound lot, Marathon Estates, Blue Hill Heights, Kim's Crescent, San Souci, Sea Breeze Estates, Millenium Gardens, Oakes Field, Misty Gardens, Hollywood Subdivision, Jasmin Gardens, Colony Village, Major's Subdivision, Sears Addition.

Streets were often gives the names or surnames of the first residences of a particular road.

SURNAMES :- Nassau is a melting pot of all the surnames found throughout the Bahamas, but, there are a few "titles" are are more common in some areas than in others.

Fox Hill :- Roker, Rahming, Brice, Edgecombe, Rolle, Burnside

Gambier :- Fernander

Bains Town :- Carter, Eneas, Nicholls, Adderley, Minus, Dean, Sweeting

Fort Hill :- Culmer, Gibson, Turnquest, Thompson

MRS TERRY ANN EVANS BAIN

Chippingham :- Symonette, Bailey, Adderley, Archers

Pyfroms Addition :- Pyfroms, Clarkes, Clyde

Bamboo Town :- Dorsettes

CHAPTER TWENTY-THREE

Gal Tell Me That Again!

E very country in the world has something that sets it apart from the others, be it language, dialect and/or social practices.

This chapter contains a collection of Bahamian words and phrases that are unique to the true, true Bahamian.

TRUE, TRUE, BAHAMIANESE

Whether you are from the old school or new school, if you don't know these words and phrases, check your birth certificate:

Ya Mah	*Musse*
Sly poke	*Slow poke*
Take the lass	*Jook*
Gatty	*Poppy show*
I inquest	*Bruggadum bam*
Gimme	*Niggerly*
Fire engine	*Spancil*
Turnover catgut	*Hoggish*
Slam bam	*Head foamus*
Well muddoes	*Stoke people up*
Terlitt	*Makecase*
Curry favour	*In da field*
Gruel	*Soon tereckley*
Dollie house	*Catch gapsee*
Robin	*Bannister rail*
Gun cassin	*Capunkled up*
Crendalin	*Clapboard house*
Buck ya toe	*They raggy her*
Warby	*No broughtupsy*
Get shanked	*Air out your clothes*
Skalawag	*Bulla*

Gritsy teeth
Moo-moo
Flit
Commolly
Flit gun
Lard
Black sambo
Glass sash
Corming
I gee
Fetch
Caul
Tingum
She ring me this morning
Swonger
No end in sight for all her troubles
Bunch up
Easier said than done
Pault with rock
Stop making all dat racket
Boom sukie boom
I ain gat one earthly thing
In cahoots with
Skylack
He tink he's all dat and a bag of chips

The current off
Titta
Stench the door
Colonkey
Stench the window
Ba bookie and ba rabbie
Clean off
Hully gully
Running round shirt-tail
Hice up
Cry baby sour lime
Rough dry
Raining cats and dogs
Spry
Batten up the house
Don't give 2 hoots
Strip bald naked
Bongey
Buggerman
Goosey
Government gate
Sperrit
Trifle
Swonger down the road
It was right on the tip of my tongue

IF YOU LAND YOURSELF IN TROUBLE

Landing yourself in trouble had major consequences. It was like you were on trial and you stood accused. The "Judge" was usually your parents or some other older person. If found guilty, you usually received the maximum penalty – and there was plenty of that for every wrongdoing. And trust, no one was above the "Parental Law"

If you heard these sayings below, you know you were being warned!

You can't sit still for nothing
All hell break loose
Don't be a market donkey
You go head and cut off your nose to spite ya face

She come gunning for me
You musse wake up on the floor
I have a bone to pick with you
You upset the apple cart

I ga knock the living daylights out ya
He scare the Bajesus out of her

Ya Mah had a holy kerniption
Youse a piece of work
I hear you was carrying on like a yard dog
Good riddance to bad rubbish
I hear you was raising cane
When they turn on you fa true

I hear you was fighting like a riffer
Why you let him gink you in ya head
She ga stomp ya guts out
You jump out the frying pan into the fire
You up to something
Youse yuck up my vexation
You up to no good
You gone push the wrong button
I'll knock you down in cold blood
She ga run up side your head

You knit picking
You wake up on the wrong side of the bed
I hear you wake up the whole neighbourhood
You had no rights being there

That's why trouble can't stay from your doorstep
She left him in da lurch
Ya friends going to land you in hot water

I don't trust you as far as I can spit

I ga knock you where the sun don't shine
Blow ya nose where you catch cold
Why you kick up such a fuss
You ga cause me lay down my three Godhead
Ya Mah ga throw a hissy - fit
I ain bailing no one out
You make ya bed hard you ga lay in it
You break up house
If you don't change dog eat ya lunch
You break up a happy home
I ain born as big as I is

Ya goose cooked
I been there and done that
You gone stir up things
I could see you up to your tricks
You gone stir up trouble
I mussie look like the thing with the 2 big ears
She ga have ya head
You really showing your true colours
You talk some and leave some

Ain't I tell you to stay from round them people place
You better learn to cool ya passion

I wasn't gonna hear the end of that
If you don't hear ya ga feel

YOU HEAR THE LATEST (GOSSIP)

If you were somebody who liked discussing other people's affairs, you were considered a 'gossip' or 'busybody'. Being a gossip or busybody was a bad thing – it was even worse if you were trying to tell something and couldn't get your 'story straight'.

189

Case in point, while in high school one of our friends told our circle something very confidential on the field during lunch break, we were sworn to secrecy. Imagine the next day to our suprise, hurt and anger we were confronted by someone outside our circle with a twisted version of what we were told the day before.

We found the culprit of the group and needless to say that ended a 5-year friendship, we wondered what other secrets were spilled by "our so-called friend".

Despite the negative connotations of being a gossip, many people were still very good at it. To be a "good" gossiper, you had to be an investigator or private eye to make sure you had the relevant facts to make the story really juicy.

Whenever somebody was either *catching gapseed* or spreading it, they would usually start with the phrase "I hear...." then be followed by one of the phrases below:

She catch him in a big lie	*Spit it out*
Hear say don't stand up in a court of law	*See like you don't see, hear like you don't hear*
Chile bite ya tongue	*I does mind my own business*
i don't get Caught up in you say, I say	*Why you sticking your nose in other peoples business*
You better watch ya mouth	*Her ears dragging on the ground listening to news*
She talking crap	*I don't poke where I don't belong*
Tell the truth and shame the devil	*You better back up what you say*
I heard it through the grapevine	*Tell her, mays well go on ZNS*
He make her eat teeth sandwich	*They ga make you swallow your words*
Slip of the tongue	*Always looking for something to talk*
Tell some tall tales	*Everything in her ear, out her mouth*
Drag my name through the mud	*She ain rest til she get the whole story*
Shut mouth, no catch flies	*She eating crow*
Pick ya mouth	*Like put her mouth up in things*
She's talk up a storm	*I positive bout dat*

She let that slip
Like tell ole stories
He tight lipped

Mum is the word
Drey load of dirty lies
A little birdie told me
Leave well enough alone
Sip - sip

Whistle and I'll point
She like tote news
Dat's too juicy to let go

Yes, no, maybe so
You talk some, and you keep some
She's lie like a riffer
How you get in that
He's talk on 2 sides of his mouth
Keep your mouth outa it

We playing catch up

Dat don't concern you
Something get up inside her head

She ger ketch in her own lie
Dey his outside children

Always digging for news
He don't know how nothing go
Watching people but ain know what gern on in her own house
Leave them hanging by a thread
Don't get me up in your business
She sure put her foot in her mouth
I ain know nuttin
She gat her nose in everyones business
Truth be told
Run ya mouth
Chile only God one knows and he ain't talking
Mouth run like water
That's an open secret
Don't know what to say
She's run right out
Talk with a double tongue
He does let anything come out his mouth
Always poking her nose where it shouldn't be
Boy she don't know what to say
Dog what bring you a bone, will carry a bone
Wasn't a bit of truth in what he said
She 2 faced bad

BAD WAYS PEOPLE (DOG WAYS)

All of us have met some really mean and miserable people ('bad ways' people) in our time. These are people who should be on another planet by themselves; but unfortunately, we had to learn to live with them.

For example, I once had a neighbor who never hesitated to ask for help or money when she needed it but would refuse to help other people when it was time to pay it forward. She had a reputation around the neighborhood for having 'bad ways'.

MRS TERRY ANN EVANS BAIN

When we talk about people having 'bad ways' or 'dog ways', we mean people like:

Talk and throw lowness in your face
Don't care how you feel
Back talking you all the time
Face always screw up
Think they slick
Would black ball you first chance they get
Don't let anything good come out of their mouth
Always rubbing someone the wrong way
Do you a dirty trick
Sly as a fox
Ducking you all the time
Like to bad mouth people
Give you a bad name
Thin skinned
Can't be trusted
Like to dig up the past
Can't trust as far as you can spit
Looking for soft spot
Outa sight, outa mind
Give me the brush off
We don't go 2 steps
Like to keep their foot on your neck
Hard headed
Stuck up

Want to hang onto you like white on rice
Don't mix
Don't hurt their head bout nothing
Kick you when you are down

Ain gat me to study
Always freaking out

Always on their tact
Can't figure them out

Always on their spell

No manners and rude

Always up in arms

Stingy
Always acting iffy
Stuck on their self
Always carrying on bad
Don't carefy

Is a snake in the grass

Thinks he's the cut above

Bite the hands that feeds them
Got plenty street smarts
Always flip flopping
Don't hurt his head
Always doing their own thing
Gets besides themselves
Don't hit it off with nobody
Thinks he's the cat meow
Acting like their head bad
Like to use people
Always showing off
Could give but they can't take
Take advantage of anybody
Play forget conveniently
Shifts like the tide
Swear or take their oath they ain't say something
Head does swing

Like to pretend they don't see you
Ain't worth five cents
Lend out your things without asking you
Is an Indian giver
Promise sincerely and never show up
You can't plant corn by their rain
Show no regard for your time or money
Living it up out of other peoples pockets
Borrow with no intention of paying back

192

Touchas
Turn their back on ya
Go back on their word
Want something in return

Like confusion
Has a tormenting spirit

Envious

Like to talk in codes

Some timish
Slight you
Two faced
Not dependable
Stand offish
Will take ya last and don't worry bout it
She's look down on her family
She forget where she came from
He ain't nuttin to depend on

Don't give 2 hoots about anyody
They only want you for what they can get from you
She only looking out for number one
She really bossy
He/she sinmaking
Underhanded
Want the whole kit and kaboodle
Can't stomach him
He's a con artist
He's a scammer
He always looking for freebies
She'll borrow your very last dime and leave you with nothing

Always letting you down
Always saying you don't need that
All for me baby
Like to plan for your time and money
Always, me, myself and I
Give them an inch they'll take a mile
So proud their foot doesn't touch the ground
Beggers can't be pickers and choosers
Likes to hurt people's feelings
Slick talks as smooth as butter
Always running right out
Stubborn as a mule
Always getting out of hand
Won't offer you time to die

He thinks he's a cut above
Always talking bad bout people
Don't hold ya breath waiting on him
He only know ya when he need ya
They'll wear you right out

She ain come from nothing

He/she troublesome
Sneaky, up to skullduggery
A trickster
Want the whole shebang
He's a schemer
He's a Flammer
She always looking for handouts
She'll take ya eye out ya head
Always rubbing you the wrong way

BAD HABITS

Most parents were intolerant of bad habits and they usually felt as if they failed as parents if these habits persisted into adulthood. The motto for them was 'bend the tree whilst it was young.'

So you never passed an adult unless you spoke, answered yes/no Mam or Sir, said excuse me, or just stepped aside as a mark of courtesy. You were threatened with a bleach and joy mouthwash for saying bad words or not telling the truth, rapped on your knuckles for teefing and a teeth sandwich for backtalking.

We often heard the following if you don't break those bad habits:

Someone ga turn the table on ya
She always pigging out

I ga turn my back on you
Don't cut your eye at me
Don't go looking for what you
didn't put down
Who you sucking your teeth at

You all capunkled up

They'll suck you dry

Ya hands too light
Like to sponge off you

I don't want you to be good for
nuttin
Duck out on ya
Don't you rack up there to cause
mischief
Swear on the Bible
He does cuss more than a manowar
sailor
Swear on dead mother's grave
Keep your head out of the clouds
Stop squackling
Don't go along with the crowd
Ya mouth hard

You buss right up
Stop cackling like a hen

Don't come here tipsy

You too play-play
You musse left your manners at
home
You does fart around
He'll teef Jesus of the cross
Don't come here pissy drunk

Only Jesus blood can take that lie
of ya
People have to sleep with one eye
open around you
He would teef thunder and catch at
lightning
You gat sticky fingers
He like a graveyard he don't refuse
nothing
Stop dribbling like a baby

Stop making all that racket
He reeling drunk

You stubborn like a mule
She worry herself to death

Don't be a fly by night
He high as a kite
I don't want you keeping company
Fight like a riffer
You are known by the company you
keep
He drunk as a skunk
Bad company corrupts good
manners
Don't make up stories

She could cart boy

He drunk as a bat
Eat you out of house and home

He soused to the gills
He ain know when last he see a sober day
When he don't bathe he smell like a mangy dog
He's get dunk to speak a sober mind
I don't want you dancing dutty round here
Falling down drunk

You ga dig your grave with your teeth
He drink to drown his sorrows
Don't have me on no wild goose chase
He's a bad pay
Youse a slacker
You ain fa real
She's talk a mile a minute
Will sell his birthright for slackness
He does drink like a fish

Don't follow fashion with everyone you meet
Lie like a cat
If he jump off the bridge you ga jump off too?
You too hot headed
Look before you leap

You like to chicken out

All you gat is your name

He'll give you dregs to drink

Bathe your skin and stop catching cowboys
Give me a sieve to drink out

Stop from being a backstabber
Like to give people the leavings

You just like a rolling stone
You always so rough dry
He is all for me baby
Keep her house like a pigpen
She loose like a goose
He's the biggest crook in town

CURRY FAVOUR

Curry favouring always gets you plenty of enemies, you were always called a blue-eyed baby. Many persons used this favour to their advantage.

The biggest disadvantage were to people who were overlooked or by-passed even though they qualified for company trips, promotions or recommendations because of the preferred one.

If you were shown some unmerited favour, expect to hear this:

You in like flint

He got the hook up

Talk in codes
You gee
Break even
By the skin of their teeth
Right on the money

Just breeze through
Suck up
Skunk the exam
Ain't what you know, but who you know
She's a brown noser
He could do no wrong in her sight
She bad out there
The sun rise and set on him

Take for granted
She'll move heaven and earth for him
Head him off at the pass
She's let him get away with murder
She ease up on her
He'll swear for him

In cahoots with them
She'll put her neck on the chopping block for him
Give him a tip off
She have him up on a pedestal
He won't let fly light on her
He's a boot licker

You may as well save your breath
She cloaks him in his wrong doing
She love the dirt he walk on
Turn a blind eye
She won't let his foot touch the ground
Put up with his foolishness
Nothing too good for her
Take up for them
He gets whatever he wants

They partners in crime
He ain know what it is to sweat
Toot him up
She ain't never had a hard day in her life
He's a brown noser
Her mother left her fixed

Bark worse than bite
She's the blue - eyed baby
She run things round here
He left everything cut and dry for her
She's a butt kisser
She ain gat nothing to worry about

Lap it up
He gat it made in a shade
She turn a blind eye to him
She does smile in ya face and stab you in da back

WORK

If you don't work you ain ga eat. Everyone had a trade, something to put bread on the table, clothes on your back and pay your bills. You had to make your own sunshine.

Having a family meant you had to find gainful steady employment or you were referred to as 'good fa nuttin'. A lot of responsible men and women took less than favourable jobs to make ends meet and to support their families.

196

In the mid 70's the airline that my father worked for closed down. The only job he could find was a supervisor at the city dump in the office. He went fishing on the weekends and my mother sold it to the neighbours along with her thriving Avon business.

Together they paid the bills and kept our family of ten clothed and fed. There is dignity in working hard and honestly.

You often heard these words:

I don't play around
Rustle up something
I does bust my gut to make ends meet
Throw together something
I down with dat
Talk is cheap, money buy land
Sometimes I can't even scratch the surface
Want to walk all over me
He ain up to par
Won't lift a finger to help
Up at the crack of dawn
It ain't over til it's over
Slim pickings
Stock up on groceries
The struggle is real
I'd rather clothe than feed ya
Go to bed with the roosters
Leave me on my own
She slunking
Leave me to fend for myself
She slacking off

There are bigger fish to fry
Build from scratch

Throw in the towel
Getting by, by the skin of your teeth
Upset the apple cart
Chile I taking it easy

Crunch time
She making a pretty penny
I down to the wire

She has butter fingers
Tings tough as nails
Push come to shove
Lounge around

My job is to emp out the garbage
Step up to the plate
Get ship shape
Gat no spunk
Belly full is a belly full
He Is a dead head
Dis place too jam-up to work
Falling down on the job
Have cake and eat it too
Don't bet on him
Tired as a dog
Don't bet your life on it
Worked my skin off
Flying down the road in the truck to work
Trying to get my feet wet
I pull masef up by my own bootstraps
He dead lazy
Working up a breeze

Work til I drop
Working up a storm

Ketch fire heap

Get the ball rolling
A dime a dozen
Every can stand on it's own bottom
One door closes, another opens
Dat's above my pay grade
Easy come, easy go
I ain't got a copper
University of hard knocks
Money don't grow on trees
Don't knock it til you tried it
All buck up goes
Fetch my hammer

Not enough to take a dent out of the bills
Try mah hand
He ain lift a finger
He just knock off from work
Put your money where your mouth is
Boss man, boss lady

Clean sweep
Making up for lost time
He good at sealing the deal
I ga bounce back, you ga see
He work so hard he running off the fumes

Hope you know what you depending on
Get crackerlacking
He always ready like Freddy
Black people time
Stitch in time saves nine
Hustle through
I work til pitch dark
Butcher up the job
Come home from work day clean
Do a botched job
Ain no such thing as a free lunch
Work til you bend
We right down to the wire and our gully picking
I can't catch ma breath for tiredness
My hands are tied
He allergic to work
You gatta save for a rainy day
Work the whole nine yards

Don't hang ya basket higher than you can reach
Easy as threading a needle
Hard work never kill nobody
These bills don't give me a break
He so tired he running out of gas
When he finish your work it's a done deal

TELL ME RIGHT OFF

This next group of sayings is self-explanatory, all it means
that the next person had the last word and you could not
rebut fast enough:

I don't roll over and play dead for no one
Up in arms
Vex as six
So mean and tight
Hog knows where to rub his skin
Ya mah turning over in her grave
You musse smell yoursef

Nose out of joint

No mah bouy
You and me ain no company
Clip ya wings
Blow off steam
No holds barred
Clear ya head

He so mad if you cut him he won't bleed
I'll out ya light
Get down to the nitty gritty
I'll knock you where the sun don't shine
Don't press your luck
You musse teef the church money
I ain no pansy
Ya mah musse pity a dog
Tongue and teeth does disagree
Raising cane
Hold him over the coals
You trying to out my light
Speak for yourself

Til hell freezes over
Put them in their place

Better ketch yasef
This little ax could cut down a big tree
Don't cause me lose my religeon
I'll make you eat your words

If the cap fits
You think you is thundereble
See ya later alligator
You is a snake in the grass
After a while crocodile
You is a pond rat
Well blow me down
You is a swamp pig
Take my head off
You gat egg on your face
Chew me right out
You can't hold a stick to her
Cut you down to size
You think you bad out there
All up in arms
She tell me off right to my teeth
I cut him down to size
He only get by, cuz he ketch me off guard

And whatcha ga do

Just like dog lost he tail
Don't talk to me like dat
Gone with her tail between her legs

Slap in the face
She take my nerves
Upset my liver
You vex take your text
Gave him a piece of my mind
Fix his business for him
Lay down my three Godhead
Eat my dust
You backing up on a b**ch punch and a sucker blow
She think she slick
You ain know who you messing with
Look like a hen hard up with egg
Don't let this nice face fool ya

Don't let the devil fool ya
You ain the only one who know bad people you know
He huffin and puffin
I gat connections
She puff right up
You could run but you can't hide
He gatta have the last word
You look like your own Grammar
You think you high and mighty
My head just as bad as yours
That's a lie from the pits of hell
I don't take things lightly
Don't get up on your hind legs nah
Just like a slap in the face
Walk around on egg shells
She was so mad she fly over here
You so full of yourself
She turn me round like an ole fool
He does throw low blows
I don't let my guard down fa long

LIFE

You only have one life to live so try and live it right. Everything you do in life whether good or bad will come back to you.

You grew up hearing these words, they sounded like a broken record but we discovered that if you live long enough it was absolutely true. Words like:

You can't do wrong in this life and get by
Take no prisoners
You is the last button on Abraham's coat
Dig one ditch, dig two

Always keep up ya birthday
Today for me, tomorrow for you

If you spit in the wind, it will come back to you
Once a man twice a child
Live good, you can live the life of Riley
Children should be seen and not heard
Pigs grow to hogs

This soon blow over
Let bygones be bygones
You can't hear you'll feel
Be surefooted

Make ya bed hard you ga lay in it

Don't make yourself a sitting duck
My hands tied
If you don't mind your lesson you will always get duck egg
Leave well enough alone
You should know better than that
They'll run circles round him
Don't burn your bridges
They really gone down nah

You have to go to God for yourself

Ya luck raw
Don't let no one rain on your parade
Just keep on living if you think you haven't seen everything
Save some for a rainy day
You can't done the world, the world will done you
If you don't have, do without

Rome wasn't built in a day
Look but don't touch

Time waits on no man

He raise his children single handedly
Some things are better left unsaid
Don't let anyone think they own ya
Loose lips, sink ships
Work hard and you never want for nothing
What man and wife discuss on their pillow stays there
You won't always see eye to eye
Don't get between man and wife
Do wrong and you will get lock up for life
Live and let live
Don't let no one walk all over you
Don't kill the messenger
Don't conk out on life
Oil and water don't mix

INSIGHTS FROM PAST BAHAMIAN GENERATIONS

What goes around comes around

Be straight laced
Dis is how we roll
Eating potcake is no disgrace
He don't know no more than the
man in the moon
Don't let him be a monkey on ya
back
Teef from teef make God smile

Don't let your left hand know what
your right hand is doing
Yuo ga see the handwriting on the
wall
Ride on your own gown tail

Play hard to get sometimes
Never say never

Go to sleep with the chickens

He running rough shod all over the
place
First rat in the hole tail covered
Like a dog lost he tail

No family when night comes

Like a chicken without a head

Bush crack, man gone
In all my born days I never se
nothing like this
Don't be so heavenly minded, you
ain no earthly good
Give him a run for his money

Don't be so quick to throw in the
towel
Eat of the fat of the land

Always stay cool as a cucumber
Leave them in God's hands
Work hard and you can live high of
the horse and sleep like a log

You need to repent in sack cloth
and ashes
You haveta crawl before you walk
You could break that family curse
What you see is what you get
Don't cry over spilled milk

Heaven help us

Don't be in hiding like a needle in a
haystack
Troubles are a dime a dozen

You need to turn over a new leaf

You don't want to work, you will
knock bout from pillar to post
Learn to stand up for yourself
The grass ain't always greener on
the other side
Put your money where your mouth
is
Ya ga be old twice as long as
you're young
No man is an island
Don't get licked with your own
stick
She will give you the clothes of her
back
Don't begrudge people for what
they have, cuz you don't know
what they had to do to get they
have
He will give you his heart
You never miss the water 'til the
well run dry
Life is a struggle

You may see the glory but don't
know the story
Help me outa scrape

Some people sacrifice their souls to
get what they want in life
He dress down to kill
Belly full is a belly full
She put on all her clothes

201

Don't kick a person when he down

Hungry belly make a man eat raw corn
Don't stomp on him when he's down
She get more than she expect out of life
You ga live long, I just call ya name
He ain use to nothing
Just starting out

He ain gat pot to piss in and window to throw it out
Don't toot your own horn

All he have is the clothes on his back
Don't let no one take you for a poppyshow
Some people only know ya when they need ya
Play with puppy they lick your mouth
He stenching on making a decision
Don't be a regular run of the mill
For all intents and purposes
This is a dog eat dog world

Your word is your bond
What you see is what you get
Sticks and stones can break my bones but calling me names won't hurt me
Dog better than ya
Don't make no promise you can't keep
He's a johnny come lately

Don't leave them hanging by a thread
Straighten up and fly right
Don't ever go back on your word
Don't take the bait

You born and bred here
Don't back down from nobody

What's in your house let it stay in your house
Good thing God ain like man

Keep your business to yasef

Lord help those who help themselves
Keep your business out da street

Don't have mammy, suck pappy
Don't let anybody put their mouth up in your business
Put God first

Run from anyone who says, "If I was you......"
Only God knows and he ain't talking
What good for the goose, ain good for the gander
Haste makes waste

The dog what bring you a bone will carry a bone
On hindsight
Always give people a chance in life
I won't hold my breath on you
Be nice cuz you could be entertaining an angel unawares
I got ya back
Always mind your manners
All disappointment for the best

Never too late to start over in life
Heaven knows best

Life always gives you a second chance
Money parts many friends

Dead men tell no tales
Look before you leap
Let people be able to take your word to the bank
All shut eye ain sleep
Ain't no such thing as a free lunch

INSIGHTS FROM PAST BAHAMIAN GENERATIONS

Close knit family
Hog know where to rub his skin
You could choose your friends, but
you can't choose your family
Poorness is no disgrace, but a big
putback
Blood thicker than water
A penny saved, is a penny earned
Can't see hide nor hair of her
You never stop learning til you die
Don't give up the fight

As long as you ain dead you ain't
pass nothing
My two feet is my car cuz I ain gat
no trans
Sickness and death is for
everybody
I have to foot it
I say what I mean, and, I mean
what I say
Be true to you
Don't let no one fool you with a
Judas kiss
Live and let live
Today for me, tomorrow for you
Wear people like a loose garment

In life, you'll either sink or swim
Don't let the devil fool ya
Keep friends close and your
enemies closer
He can't win for losing
Sense and manners take you
through the world
You ain carrying nothing with you
All that glitters is not gold

Don't overdo everything,
If you live to get old, you will be
old twice as long as you were
young
Sometimes it's best to leave well
enough alone
We will cross that bridge when we
get there

Now you cooking with gas
Don't bite the hands that feed you
Don't be high minded

What you give to the world you
can't take back
Younce is younce
Sometimes you can't win for losing
Better health than wealth
In life you gatta ketch sense fast
Don't bite off more than you can
chew
Things going good he in dog
heaven
Poor as a church mouse

Time brings on changes

Lay down the law
This a give and take life

Always save for a rainy day
Don't put your mouth in things that
don't concern you
What goes around comes around
Don't take people on
Those who criticise you will be the
first to condemn you
Ise a no-nonsense person
Don't fall prey to the devil
Karma is a b***h

There's nothing new under the sun
What goes around, comes around

Live to live again
If you wan know me come live with
me
You only live once, make it count
Don't let anyone make you stoop to
their level

You gotta learn to hold your peace

Be never too big to say sorry

RELATIONSHIPS

Everyone is your family or far off cousin or know your peoples them. Neighbours became close kin mainly because you had to depend on them if your relatives were far away.

We looked out for each others homes, children and yard. Great relations were formed and there was a lasting bond. Not all were good and you have to take the good with the bad. They would:

Treat you like their own
She get more than she expected
Keep an eye out for you
He won't let fly light on her

Blood thicker than water
Don't respect God or man
Some family would say, I ain getting in that
He baby struck
Some would say he keeping sweetheart
Chile you ain want no part of them
She two timing him
She's got mothers wit

He ain no one to trust
He still have milk around his mouth
He get roach on his bread
Rob the cradle
They set you up
Harbour slackness'

Some don't know how far to go
She marry her faddah
Put up a front
They have their Pah boxing bout the place
He look like the very man

They treat her like a queen
Family can't hide

They treat him like a king
Ya mah ain't lie on your pa

I don't get in no one way
Just like we is strangers
She really slack
You won;t believe we from the same Mah and Pah
She's a hot potato
They cut from a different cloth
She so bad she break down jericho wall
They does treat me like a stepchild
She stubborn as a mule

They don't give us the time of day
She head over heals in love
You won't believe we grow up eating out the same pot
Her head in the clouds
I fall down and get up with them
Cousins make dozens
My family turn their back on me
Turn his world upside down
They treat me so good I ain want for nutting
She looking for man
They is take care of me good
He marry his muddah
She's the spitting image of her ma

They is treat me better than my own family
What you see is what you get
My family only looking out for what they can get
Can't judge a book by it's cover
My family don't check for me

204

She does play me too close
I don't keep company

God charge you for breaking up a happy home
Thin line bewteen love and hate

She so glad he gone she hice a flag

A man who cheat with you will cheat on you
Let her eat her heart out

I keeps to myself
My family don't know if I living or dead
That's why I don't keep company

I don't know the last day I see or hear from them
Men rarely marry women who they run around with
She's truck too much

He always dressed down from head to toe

WHAT YOU THINK I IS ??

You had better know how you stepping up when you come to me, I don't play that. You best come straight or don't come at all, I don't skylack.

You don't talk to me any kind of how! Step back Jack! When addressing or talking to people be very careful not to 'get right out ya skin' like the older folks would say. You had to step light and proper or you were put in 'ya place'.

What or who you think I is?:

Tingum in the bush ain't gat no name
I ain no Small fry
Youse run me up on brakes
Andros crab catcher
You in the dog house
Long Island sheep runner
Hit the ground running
Off your rocker
I musse look like a market donkey
Sharp as a tack

I ain no stick in the mud
Rock the house
The chip don't fall far from the block
Take over the conversation
You'll cut off the same block

Head white as snow

Hate him like poison
Show all your teeth
Catch the hint
Write like foul scratch
Tickled pink
You fooling yourself
Pleased as punch
You cheesing
I musse look like the thing with the two big ears
I is old school
He go for bad
You gat me on edge

Youse get carried away
I ain ga take it to heart

205

MRS TERRY ANN EVANS BAIN

You surely could fool me
You'll just like two peas in a pod
Live like no tomorrow
She scared of him like the devil
scared of holy water
Youse show right off
You ain no better than me
You don't know what to say
Every rope has an end
Stuck in the mud
Give you enough rope to hang
yourself
Dead weight
I ain't in y'all business
Where your mind is
I ain easily led
He space out
They have airs about them
Don't know his head from his tail
Take for granted
Don't know when conch done
You brassy eye
Don't know A if it was as big as his
head
Don't jerk me around
He don't make a bit of sense
Knock him over with a feather
She tingsey
Blow me down

He gets carried away
You need to turn over a new leaf
You musse crazy
You need to be on the pink porch

You ain't gat no guts

He duncy
You ain't gat no balls
She topsy turvy
Off the hizzy fa shizzy

She from the crazy hill
Time longer than rope
You reap what you sow
She living on a wing and a prayer
No skin off my teeth
Well mudda take sick

He's a fly by night
You making sport
He ain gat me to study
You drawing a blank

Talking to her is like pulling teeth
Your mind is in a fog
She Holier than thou
Ain't no such thing as a free lunch
He scatter brained
Live by the sword, die by the
sword
She's a numbskull
Play with dogs you have fleas
Stupid is as stupid does
You shoot yourself in the foot
The frog say correct
Early bird catch the first worm
You triffulling
Pay him no mind
You ain't serious
Sight for sore eyes
You need to back down

Long time no see
You need to back over
Look like come here lemme fix ya
You don't know your place
Look like something the cat
dragged in
You power hungry
Run for ya life
You set in your ways
She'll give you a run for your
money
You can't teach an old dog new
tricks
Up in Fox Hill Hilton
You done wear out your welcome
I don't do monkey business
You stay there showing all your
teeth
Once in a blue moon
You think you gat the winning edge
He live way behind God's back
Youse a smarty pants
Ain't got no gumption
My hands full

206

Mellow like a fellow	*He think he's a cool dude*
You ain ga make me no scapegoat	*Ya head does swell*
No more sense than a land curb	*If you tell the truth you don't need*
	a good memory
He's a hard nut to crack	*He better get outta my sight*
She makes me sick	*He makes my skin crawl*
He want be all over me like flies on	*I don't do that sweethearting thing*
a fish	
I musse look hard up	*He musse think I desperate or*
	sumtin

FEELINGS

Catching feelings is something everyone goes through at one time or another, but, some people could give but they can't take. They have no problem cutting you down but they can't take the blows.

I had a coworker who had no problem telling anyone about how they looked or apparel was too tight or hair looked bad. One day she came to work with a poor make-up job, no one had the nerve to tell her.

She went to the restroom and while washing her hands she saw how awful she looked. She fussed everyone out for not telling her, and, then became vex and aloof the rest of the day.

It was a no-win situation, either way, she would have been mad.

These punches are below the belt:

I ga spit on your grave	*He seeing the man*
You musse think you is man	*She screw me over*
You ain't gat no where to go	*His gully picking*
You musse think you is woman	*She's a fun sucker*
I ga dance on your grave	*He seeing stars*
Every married man has his own	*Running bout helter- skellter*
bonefish	
She's as happy as a lark	*He smell rancy*

The same people you meet going
up, you ga meet them same people
coming down
He's happy go lucky
She having a senior moment
What goes around comes around
It's as clear as mud
Don't bite the hand that feeds you
I see said the blind man
You fit a good cut hip

Age ain't nothing but a number
You ga get the licking stick

Devil may care
You crazy, ain't a shadow of a
doubt
Work hard but don't play hard
Penny for your thoughts

She blow me right out the water

He ain too copasetic
On pins and needles
Dead men tell no tales

Come too late you broke the plate
Put that baby to rest
You ain gat no heart
God ga strike you down
What's done in darkness will come
to light
He was gone in a flash
She wear her heart on her sleeve
You ain't no mover or shaker
He does dress to impress

I can't stand her
I too good fa dat
She hate him like poison
She too good for him

You too pig-headed
She too grudgeful

He stubborn as a mule
He can't be trusted
I tired of talking to you

What sweet ya mouth, bitter ya tail

Good riddance to bad rubbish
All that glitters ain't gold
By hook or crook
Give with both hands open
Foot to foot behind me
Church out, crab crawling
You have to tiptoe around her
feelings
She shame-faced
You gat to walk on egg shells
around her
Knock me off my feet
I love ya cuz ya decent

I won't hold my breath for you
He ain't gat a decent bone in his
whole body
Walk around with his head in the
clouds
One day at a time
She crying her eyes out
Sense and manners take you
through the world
She had her heart set on it
Dogs don't bark at parked cars
Between a rock and a hard place
Delayed but not denied
She wish she coulda crawl under a
rock
Make ya bed hard you ga lay in it
This weather kicking up
It's the gospel truth
She was hoping the earth would
open and swallow her up
You too like to follow fashion
I ain like how she hail me
Some funniness going on
She don't know them from here to
binks
You bluffing
Her feelings hurt over every little
thing
You joking right
You better make page of your age
Youse a jive turkey

He is a boot licker

I talk to her till I blue in the face
You better scatter like batter
You musse shake hands with the devil
I beg your pardon
You ga bust hell wide open
Get down to the nitty gritty
Youse a simple simon
Get down to brass tacks
I swear on a stack of Bibles
It just dawn on me
He think he is the smartest thing in Skin
She thinks the sun rise and set on him
Tit for tat, butter for fat
You gatta try to bring up the rear

Carry your big guram (belly)
Dog better than him
Wide eyed and bushy tail
All fun done
He seeing the pearly gates
She really high minded

She like throw lowness
He like crack jokes

Squash out clothes
You can't bite the hands that feed them
Listen before you speak
She niggerly
He gat niggeritis
Favour ain't fair
She had an old age pension baby
A penny for your thoughts
I hopping but I ain stopping

Listen to older people, eye winker was here before beard
Take it from an old fool
Chile I over and done with that
He's a sitting duck

He vengeful
Back in the day
Ya goose cooked
That's your headache
I get a sinking feeling bout that
I ain't getting in dat
She does go with the tide
Living high of the horse

She troubling my spirit

I don't give two hoots
Something ain't right but I can't put my finger on it
He skunk them
Common sense ain't common
When powerful be merciful
Age before beauty
He does look down on people
Chile she's a 'all for me baby' kinda person
Like look down on people
When ya get bad ways, dog better than ya
Just like 2 peas in a pod
Don't jump the gun

They skinge on the food
She hoggish
They think they have arrived
My mind don't lead me wrong
I feeling fine and dandy
I am too Blessed to be stressed
People may not remember what you say, but they won't forget how you treat them.

GLOSSARY

Bahamianese / Queen's English

Ain / Don't

Alla / All of

Asue hand or draw / Weekly or monthly savings held by 1 person

Bark cocoanut / Removing the outer hard shell of a cocoanut

Bubby / The breasts

Bouy / An expression used for everything

Bookers / Long horns of the male goat

Belly / Stomach

Brazen / Very forward behaviour in a young girl

Back -back / 1) Reverse 2) Move backward

Biggerty / Someone who is strong-willed and aggressive

Bridle / Dried up secretions around the mouth

Binah / A very fat woman

Bumica head / Some one with a large protruding forehead

B. B. eyes / Hardened secretions in the corner of your eyes

Caul / Amniotic membrane over face at birth

Cut hip / Punishment using a belt or other objects

Coppit / A parcel of land that has sunken areas

Ain't / Is not

Akimba / Arms flexed in a tight bow on both sides

Bad pay / Someone who borrows money and does not pay it back

Breaking wind / Pass flatus Bout / 1) about; 2) a sudden spell of sickness

Bloomers / Oversized panties made of flour bags

Buck / Stub your foot or toe

Broughtupsey / No upbringing

Breed / 1) Pregnant   2) Having children

Black sambo / Someone who is very dark-skinned

Badevil / 1) the devil   2) evil spirit

Bleachout face / 2 colour skin tones on the face

Buggerman man / 1) Dried up snot in the nose; 2) A very ugly person

Bush crack / Loud rustling of a bush or shrub

Back talk / Answering an adult in a rude manner while they are talking to you

Crazy hill / Mental institution

Commolly bump / A large lump on the forehead following a fall or blow

Current / 1) Electricity   2) The tide

Clear ma head / 1) Time spent with oneself to think things over; 2) The sex act

Calm head / Someone who head is very flat at the back

Chile / Child (you are about to hear something juicy)

Cloak / To enable someone in wrongdoing

Cheesing / Pants sucked in the buttocks

Corming / Walking in a cute fashion

Colonkey / Oversized objects

Changes (the) / Menopause

Capunkled / All messed up

Chirren / Children

Dat / That

Dutty / Dirty

Dash / Throw down in a fight

Day clean / Very early in the morning

Don't carefy / Someone who shows little care for anyone

Dern / A mild form of swearing

Dey / They

Ebb tide / When the tide is getting low or going out

Forward / Aggressive

Fah / For

Forky teeth / Long protruding teeth

Gruel / Yellow corn meal and wheat cooked together

Flo tide / When the tide is coming in

Frill lip / Lips that are always pursed

Gapsee / Listening to gossip

Gat / Got, gotten

Gumption / Plenty nerves

Gritsy / Teeth that have a film on from poor hygiene

Gaul / Shameless aggression

Conchy Joe / Someone with very light skin but not considered to be white

Crack / 1) Loud sound; 2) Silence; 3) Sunrise; 4) Woman's private part

Curry favour / Show special favour to someone often underserved

Copacetic / You are managing well

Can cutter / Can opener

Cuz / Because

Cahoots / In agreement with

Cascating / Vomiting

Coulda / Could have

Da / The

Duncy / Very dumb

Dis / This

Dingy / Clothes discoloured from improper washing

Do 'bear' / Long out your tongue at someone

Dun / Something already done

Doting / A very forgetful person

Dere / Their

Faddah / Father

Follow fashion / Mimic an action

4 day in da morning / 4 o'clock in the morning

Frop / Hug in a rough manner

Fester / 1) Pus; 2) Rile up

Flour pap / A paste made with white flour and water

Ferl / Foil paper

Granny / A woman who delivers babies

Grabbalicious / Someone who hoards all for themselves

Ga / Going to

Gussiemae / A very stout lady

Gun cassen / Wide upper thighs

211

Government gate / 4 upper front teeth are missing

Gunning / Long pants that have gotten too short

Gattee / I don't have to do it

Gonna / Going to

Hog sty / A large pimple between the eyes

Hip shot / Walking as if one leg is shorter than the other

Hully - gully / A man who is a playboy

Hoggish / Very greedy

Honkey - dorey / Everything is in order

Hard-up / Has a need

Hesef / Himself

Hissy - fit / An adult tantrum

In - straw / Up to 6 weeks after having a baby

Iron donkey / A bicycle

Jook / Stab

Ketch / Catch

Kitty / Small cash flow

Luck raw / You are out of luck

Lard / Solid shortening oil

Lowness / Someone who constantly reminds you of a favour

Lay on my chest / Indigestion

Ma health / Menstrual period

Muddah / Mother, any older woman

Moo - moo / Short very wide dress

Miff / Angry with

Mussee / Must be

Nuttin / Nothing

Outta / Out of

Old story / Repeating old tales

Playing the throne / Ducking school

Purge / Let your feelings out

Pornch / Big round stomach

Pault / Throw rocks with a force

Gimme / Give me

Goosey / An obscene gesture at someone's rear end

Gern / Going to

Heffin / To enable in wrongdoing

Hitch up / Clothes not fitting neatly or properly

Hice up / 1) Raise the sail on a boat; 2) Clothes tucked up in certain areas

Hutt, Huttin / Hurt, hurting

Hizzy - fa - shizzy / Over the top

Hacker / Car used as taxi

Having the fits / Epilepsy

Head foamus / Landing on your head

Iffy / Uncertain

I gee / I give up

Joneser / A hard drug user

Junegalick / Dishaevelled appearance

Ketch masef / Take a break

Knead bread / Making bread from scratch

Lemme / Let me

Lock jaw / Tetanus

Life water / Intravenous fluid

Making sport / Making fun of

Makecase / Make haste, hurry up

Moo / Dance move

Muck / Make a mess of

Muddoes / Expression of suprise

Mah / Your mother

Niggerly / Very greedy

Ole / Old

On edge / 1) Nervous; 2) Sensitive

Piss / Pass urine

Peasy / Unruly hair

Plait / 1) Comb and twist hair; 2) Twine dried straws together

Poppy - show / Make a spectacle of

212

Potcake / 1) Layer of rice at bottom of pot; 2) Common name for yard dogs

Piece Meal / Paying in installments

Rig up / Dressed ridiculously

Ragged / Worn out

Runaround / Permisscuous person

Run hot / Make angry

Slick / Crafty

Slop pail or bucket / Bucket used inside the house for passing urine/faeces

Stoke up / To insult

Sticky fingers / Someone who steals

Switcha / Lemonade

Swing / Tricked into something

Spancil / To restrain someone

Sly poke / To ridicule in a playful way

Study / Not paying attention to

Starve gut / Always hungry

Seedy / 1) Crafty; 2) Unruly hair

Sometimish / Very moody

Skylack / Not serious at all

Spillagating / Fun on the town

Shank / Hit on your ankle with a rock

Stretching ma legs / Going for a walk

Trapsy / Not one to trust

Thunderebel / One who thinks he's feared

Tote or totter / One famous for carting away things from a function

Teeth pull / Tooth extracted

The lass / The last blow in any fight

Teef / Thief

Poor mouth / Someone always claiming they are broke

Queens english / Proper English

Riffer / A dangerous liar

Ring (Phone) / Call by phone

Rough dry / Unironed or unpressed clothes

Rice balow / Cooked rice with pink colour

Slunking / Procrastinating

Swonger / To walk in a proud manner

Stench the door / To use an object to keep the door open

Sweet mouth / Someone who likes meats and sweet baked goods

Slam - bam / Sausage and bread sandwich

Skullduggery / Underhanded dealings

Shifty / Can't be trusted

Slapdash / Don't do properly

Sef / Self

Smoogly / Ugly

Set / 1) Prepare to cook; 2) Good financial standing

Sic / Rile up dog at someone

Squat diddly / Not worth anything

Squashing out / Washing out clothes lightly

Sausage lips / Very full thick lips

Throwing jeers / Making unkind comments

Ting / Anything

Trifle / Not serious

Top / Palm leaves used in straw-work

Tingum / Used to describe anything or person you can't remember

Tingumsirmarybob / Unreasonable situation

Tereckley / In a little while

MRS TERRY ANN EVANS BAIN

Turnover catgut / Full body spinover

The runs / Diarrhoea

Tingsey / Materialistic

Touchas / 1) Easily offended; 2) Touching in a groping manner

Terlitt / Room off from house used to urinate and pass faeces

Underhanded / Can't be trusted

Wan / Want

Whapped out / Strung out on drugs

Younce / It is yours to have

Ya / Your

Yasef / Yourself

Yinna / You all

Ya run / Your business

Throw crop / Die

Turnout / 1) Get infected; 2) Show up in large numbers

Trifulling / Not serious about anything

Trotters / Feet of animals

Uppity / Full of pride

Warby / Type of bread made in frying pan

Whatless / Not worth anything

You gee / Do you give up

Youse / You is, you are

Yuck / 1) Take forcefully; 2) To anger

Y'all / You all

Ya Pah / Your Father

Ya tail / Your buttocks

214

Acknowledgements

I am deeply grateful to my children who have supported this project from its inception. Thank you to my son, Mr. Wilfred Bain Jr., for his meticulous work as chief editor and proof reader, and to my daughters, Mrs. Krystal Bain-Symonette and Miss Brittany Bain, for their editorial expertise and attention to detail.

Special thanks to my son-in-law, Mr. Ian Symonette, whose talents as photographer and graphic artist brought visual beauty to these pages.

To have my children so deeply involved in preserving our family's legacy and Bahamian values has made this book all the more meaningful, and I am forever grateful for their unwavering support.

About the Author

Terry Ann Evans-Bain was born in 1958 to the parents of Walter and Violet Evans (both deceased). She is the eldest of 8 children. Her childhood years, which were happy, were spent in South Beach Estates, surrounded by Grandparents and lots of extended family members. She looked forward to funerals, weddings and parties, all held pleasant and precious memories.

Church was and still is an integral part of her life. A lifelong member of Emmanuel Gospel Chapel, she, along with all of her siblings still attend Emmanuel Gospel Chapel and are active serving members.

At the age of 11 she entered the prestigious Government High School with 4 other siblings following suit. Upon completion of Senior High School, she entered the Bahamas School of Nursing; successfully becoming a Registered Nurse. Four years later, she became a Registered Midwife. She had kept on the cutting edge of her profession by embracing every opportunity for improvement by attending courses, workshops, seminars and lectures and obtained many awards and accolades. She retired in 2018 serving 43 years in a job that brought her enjoyment, fulfillment and a sense of purpose to her life. Her impact on her profession and the people she managed and served was aptly celebrated at her retirement ceremony in May 2018 wholly planned by her colleagues.

In 1975, she met Wilfred Bain, a young carpenter who joined her church shortly after his conversion. Their relationship blossomed and, in 1983, they were married. This union lasted 37 happy years until Wilfred's passing in 2020 after a brief illness. Having both retired, the last few years that Terry and Wilfred spent together demonstrated a "good life" and included travelling on short term mission trips, cruising and chillaxing. They successfully raised their 3 children, Wilfred Jr. - an Attorney at Law, Krystal (Symonette) - a Medical Technologist and Brittany - an Exercise Physiologist.

Although both parents are deceased, Terry, all of her siblings and their offspring meet frequently for family gatherings as every occasion is call for a celebration.

Generally, Terry's life is very busy as she is also a senior Choir member, Sunday School teacher, Youth Group leader, part of her church's Medical team, a mentor in the Ministry at PACE (a program for reaching young pregnant girls), a teacher for the Good News Clubs at 2 Primary Schools, an executive board member of the Retired Nurses Guild, a participant in short term mission trips to Family islands, a member of the Neighbourhood Association and a member of a Backyard Farming Group.

Terry's hobbies include music, travelling, family togetherness and spending time outdoors.

The road to writing this book started in the 1980's when Terry wrote a song for a National Competition but never submitted it, this began her start of collecting original Bahamian sayings and practices that only a "true- true" Bahamian could identify with.

During the pandemic when everything and everyone was on "lockdown", Terry was encouraged by her husband and children to put her thoughts and plans for this book in writing. When her husband passed, everything came to a halt, but her children were convinced that her completing this work would be therapeutic and help the healing process.

The main objective of this book is to share insight into the life, experiences of those wonderful happy times. To preserve our colloquial language that set Bahamians apart from the rest of the world. To encourage and foster that "lost" respect for others, especially our older people, listening and learning from them and garnering close family ties. As the stories are told and imparted in this book, it is hoped that the wisdom, trust in God and gratitude for life and all it's blessings would be appreciated.

WE ARE A BLESSED NATION BAHAMAS!

Also by the Author

The Road I've Trod: Legacy of Wisdom (Volume Two)

A heartfelt reflection on faith, family, and timeless values, offering wisdom and guidance rooted in Bahamian Christian traditions.

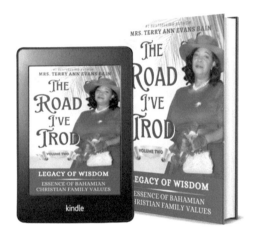

Available in Ebook, Paperback and Hardback from Amazon.

UNIVERSAL IMPACT PRESS